THE AMERICAN BAR ASSOCIATION

GUIDE TO

FAMILY LAW

*The Complete and Easy Guide
to the Laws of Marriage,
Parenthood, Separation,
and Divorce*

Copyright © 1996 by the American Bar Association

All rights reserved under International and Pan-American Copyright Conventions. Published in the United States by Times Books, a division of Random House, Inc., New York, and simultaneously in Canada by Random House of Canada, Limited, Toronto.

Library of Congress Cataloging-in-Publication Data

The American Bar Association guide to family law : the complete and easy guide to the laws of marriage, parenthood, separation, and divorce. — 1st ed.
    p.   cm.
  Includes index.
  ISBN 0-8129-2791-5 (pbk.)
  1. Domestic relations—United States—Popular works. I. American Bar Association.
KF505.Z9A47 1996
346.7301'5—dc20
[347.30615]   95-52854

Design by Robert Bull Design

Manufactured in the United States of America

9 8 7 6 5 4 3 2

First Edition

AMERICAN BAR ASSOCIATION

■

Robert A. Stein, *Executive Director*

Sarina A. Butler, *Associate Executive Director,*
Communications Group

Mabel C. McKinney-Browning, *Director,*
Division for Public Education

Charles White, *Series Editor*

PRINCIPAL AUTHOR

Jeff Atkinson
Adjunct Professor
DePaul University College of Law
Chicago, Illinois

REVIEWERS

Howard Davidson
ABA Center for Children and
the Law
Washington, D.C.

Linda Elrod
Washburn University School
of Law
Topeka, Kansas

Diane Geraghty
Loyola University School of Law,
Chicago
Chicago, Illinois

Lynne Z. Gold-Bikin
Immediate Past Chair, ABA
Family Law Section
Norristown, Pennsylvania

Lowell K. Halverson
Attorney at Law
Mercer Island, Washington

Victoria Ho
Asbell, Coleman & Ho
Naples, Florida

Burton S. Hochberg
Schiller, DuCanto, and Fleck
Chicago, Illinois

Antoinette Sedillo Lopez
University of New Mexico
School of Law
Albuquerque, New Mexico

Robert Nye
John Marshall Law School
Chicago, Illinois

Marcia O'Kelly
University of North Dakota
School of Law
Grand Folks, North Dakota

Peggy L. Podell
Podell & Podell
Milwaukee, Wisconsin

Norman N. Robbins
Robbins & Robbins
Bingham Farms, Michigan

Arnold H. Rutkin
Rutkin & Effron, P.C.
Westport, Connecticut

Dee M. Samuels
Samuels, Shawn & Marx
San Francisco, California

Phillip Schwartz
Schwartz, Ellis, and Moore
Arlington, Virginia

Patricia Garity Smits
Attorney at Law
Morristown, New Jersey

Jesse C. Trentadue
Suitter, Axland, Armstrong &
Hanson
Salt Lake City, Utah

CONTENTS

FOREWORD

■

Hilarie Bass, *Chair*
ABA Standing Committee on Public Education

T HE LAW AFFECTS each of us in our daily lives—when we send our kids to school, take the car in for repair, use a credit card, make a purchase, or go to work. If we don't understand how law governs our rights and responsibilities, we're at a considerable disadvantage in today's America.

That is the purpose of *The American Bar Association Legal Guides*—to explain the law to you in simple, easy-to-understand language. These books are concise and straightforward. By avoiding legal jargon and technicalities, they discuss in everyday words how the law affects you at home, at work, and at play. Best of all, these books will help you to avoid legal problems, to identify those that you may have, and to determine which legal problems you can solve on your own and which require the assistance of an attorney.

These books help you understand the important legal issues about marriage, separation, and divorce. They explore the legal aspects of owning a home, and the world of contracts, big and little. They tell you what you need to know to plan your estate and save money for yourself and your loved ones. They even provide guidance on planning for disability, and on end-of-life issues.

These books are organized so you can easily find what you need to know. Brief articles giving additional information on topics of great interest appear alongside the text. You will also find information about state laws, as well as about federal laws that apply across the United States.

No book can answer all the questions you might have on the law. To help you find additional help, sections at the end of each book tell you where to get more information. These sections refer you to many free or inexpensive publications, and suggest services that government agencies, bar associations, and other groups can provide at either minimal or no cost.

When reading *The American Bar Association Legal Guides,* please keep some important points in mind. First, these books cannot and do not pretend to provide legal advice. Only a lawyer who understands the facts of your particular case can do that. Although every effort has been made to present material that is as up-to-date as possible, laws can and do change.

Thus, these books should be considered an introduction to the law in each area. They are not the final word. If you are thinking about pursuing any legal action, consult first with a lawyer, bar association, or lawyer referral service to assure yourself of knowledgeable assistance. Armed with the knowledge and insights provided in *The American Bar Association Legal Guides,* you can be confident that the legal decisions you make will be in your best interests.

Hilarie Bass is in private practice in Miami, Florida. She is past president of the Florida Bar Foundation and a past member of the Board of Governors of the American Bar Association.

PREFACE

■

Robert A. Stein, *Executive Director*
American Bar Association

T HE AMERICAN BAR ASSOCIATION LEGAL GUIDES are designed to provide guidance for people on important legal questions they encounter in everyday life. When American families are asked to describe their legal needs, the topics that come up repeatedly are housing, personal finance, family and domestic concerns (usually in conjunction with divorce and child support), wills and estates, and employment-related issues. In addition, more and more Americans have questions about operating a business, often out of the home.

These are the topics that *The American Bar Association Legal Guides* cover in plain, direct language. We have made a special effort to make the books practical, by using situations and problems you are likely to encounter. The goal of these books is to give helpful information on the range of options that can be used in solving everyday legal problems, so that you can make informed decisions on how best to handle your particular question.

The American Bar Association wants Americans to be aware of the full range of options available when they are confronted with a problem that might have a "legal" solution. The Association has supported programs to eliminate delay in the courts, and has worked to promote fast, affordable alternatives to lawsuits, such as mediation, arbitration, conciliation, and small claims court. Through ABA support for lawyer referral programs and pro bono services (where lawyers donate their time), people have been able to find the best lawyer for their particular case and have received quality legal help within their budgets.

The American Bar Association Legal Guides discuss all these alternatives, suggesting the wide range of options open to you. We hope that they will help you feel more comfortable with the law and will remove much of the mystery from the legal system.

Several hundred members of the Association have contributed to *The American Bar Association Legal Guides*—as authors and as reviewers who have guaranteed the guides' accuracy. To them—and to the ABA's Standing Committee on Public Education, which was the primary force behind the publications—I express my thanks and gratitude, and that of the Association and of lawyers everywhere.

Robert A. Stein is executive director of the American Bar Association. He was formerly dean of the University of Minnesota Law School.

PREFACE

GUIDE TO

FAMILY
LAW

INTRODUCTION

■

Jeff Atkinson, member, ABA Family Law Section Council

FAMILY LAW has been evolving for about as long as human be-ings have been evolving.

When people lived together in tribes without formal govern-ments, they developed their own customs or adopted rules from their deities. In Western culture, particularly after the Norman Conquest in 1066, regulation of marriage and divorce was placed initially in the hands of the church. As church and state grew more separate, civil courts and legislatures took over more of the regula-tion of family law.

Some may wish for simpler times, when a man and woman—without any paperwork or outside officials—could be married by exchanging promises to be husband and wife from that moment on. Divorce in certain cultures and times could be simpler too. A Pueblo woman could divorce her husband by placing his moccasins outside their doorstep.

As time passed and we became more "advanced," the rules of family law became more complicated (although there are periodic legislative reforms to simplify the rules).

The goal of this book is to explain the rules.

Special attention is given to the laws of divorce, particularly the factors judges consider when deciding issues of property, alimony, child support, custody, and visitation. The book also covers other types of family law, such as the requirements of getting married, rights of persons living together, and procedures for adoption.

Family law, also known as matrimonial law or the law of domes-tic relations, often involves a great deal of stress. When people need information on family law, it is usually because they are going through—or considering—significant changes in their lives, such as divorce or separation. Other types of family law, including requirements for getting married and adopting a child, are associated with happier events but have their share of stresses too.

Knowledge of the law does not eliminate all the anxieties that may accompany a legal issue, but it is a step in the right direction. Much of the tension that people feel in a legal dispute comes from not knowing what to expect or what the options are.

This book will enable you to gain a greater understanding of the rights and responsibilities of people who are married, divorced, or living together. In addition, the information may help you work with others (including your attorney) to resolve disputes and plan for the future.

As will be noted periodically throughout this book, laws vary from state to state, and courts within a state may even decide a particular issue in different ways. For specific analysis of the law in your state, you should consult an attorney within your state who is experienced in family law.

CHAPTER ONE

■

Living Together

THE U.S. CENSUS BUREAU REPORTS that in 1990, there were 3,042,642 households consisting of an unmarried man and an unmarried woman living together. That compares with 51,718,214 households with wives and husbands living together.

LEGALITY OF LIVING TOGETHER

There is nothing illegal about an unmarried couple living together. The couple generally can live wherever they wish. Some local zoning laws prohibit more than three unrelated persons from living together in one house or apartment, but those laws would not apply to a two-person household. The government's attempt to limit a couple's right to live together would probably be considered a violation of the couple's **right to free association** under the First Amendment to the United States Constitution.

A few states still have laws on the books prohibiting **fornication**—sexual relations between two persons who are not married—but such laws are almost never enforced. Some states also have laws against **sodomy**, which, among other things, prohibit sexual relations between people of the same sex. Those laws are rarely enforced if the conduct is private, consensual, and between adults (although in 1986, the United States Supreme Court in a divided decision did uphold a Georgia law criminalizing private sexual relations between two men).

AGREEMENTS TO SHARE EXPENSES OR PROPERTY

Generally, if it is legal for two persons who are not living together to enter into an agreement, it also is legal for the couple living together to enter into a similar agreement. The fact that two people are living together and unmarried does not make an agreement automatically illegal. So, if two people wish to agree about how much each will pay for rent, mortgage, utilities, groceries, auto expenses, et cetera, the agreement can be valid and enforceable. If one party does not keep his or her end of the bargain, that person can be sued.

If the loss of a large amount of money is involved, a lawsuit or threat of a lawsuit may be worthwhile. If the dollar amount is relatively small, the wiser course of action probably is to walk away, hopefully with some added wisdom for dealing with the next relationship. Similarly, if there is no practical way to collect the amount due from the person who broke a promise—if, for example, the person has virtually no assets and no steady source of income—a lawsuit is not likely to be worth the effort.

In some cases, an unmarried couple may be considered to have a business relationship as well as a personal relationship. The combined relationship can create legal rights. In an Oregon case, for example, an unmarried couple agreed to operate a ranch together and share equally in the profits and expenses of running the ranch. When the couple split up, the partner who did not own the ranch was found to be entitled to an amount of money equal to one half of the increase in value of the ranch during the time the couple lived together and worked together.

As with any contract, if a person wants protection, it is best to make the agreement specific and in writing. An oral agreement might be enforceable, but it is much harder to prove.

In order to be valid, contracts usually need to have **consideration**. That means each party to the agreement should give some benefit to the other party, such as agreeing to pay a portion of expenses. If an agreement looks as though it is only creating a gift from one party to the other with the recipient giving nothing in return, the agreement might not be enforceable because of lack of consideration. For examples of enforceable and unenforceable agreements, see pages 8 and 9.

A PROMISE OF "I'LL TAKE CARE OF YOU"

Lawyers and judges often refer to certain agreements as "pillow talk." The couple may be in bed enjoying a moment of intimacy, but one member of the couple feels insecure about the future. The other member of the couple offers reassurance along the lines of: "Don't worry. I love you. I'll take care of you. Everything will be okay." Sometime later, everything is not okay. One member of the couple decides to end the relationship, and the more vulnerable partner does not feel taken care of at all.

If a person files a lawsuit to collect on the promise, is she or he likely to succeed?

No.

To begin with, such agreements rarely are in writing, so they are hard to prove in court.

Second, a promise that "I'll take care of you . . . Everything will be okay" is probably too vague to be enforceable. The court does not have a clear standard to determine the meaning of "take care" and "everything will be okay." In the absence of a clear agreement between the parties, courts are reluctant to create more definite terms of a contract. The quoted promise is not nearly as specific as an agreement to pay half the rent or to share equally the profits and expenses of running a ranch.

Third, even if the promise did not fail for lack of specificity, it could be viewed as contingent on circumstances that are no longer in effect. If the promise means anything, it probably means, "I'll support you financially as long as we are living together." So if the couple breaks up, a court probably would not find an enforceable promise for continued support.

Fourth, there could be a problem with consideration. As discussed in the last section, contracts usually require each party to give something in order for there to be a valid agreement. Here, the promise might be viewed as one-way or gratuitous. One partner promised to take care of the other, but there was not a specific promise in return. Therefore, the agreement could be unenforceable for that reason as well.

The partner who is seeking support might argue that he or she promised to maintain the home and provide emotional support in exchange for a promise of being taken care of. A promise of taking care of a home and providing emotional support is not likely to be specific enough to be enforceable, and it may be viewed as contingent on continuation of the relationship.

In addition, if a court thinks an agreement amounts to providing financial support in exchange for sexual relations, the court will not enforce it. Such an agreement will be viewed as uncomfortably close to a contract for prostitution.

Courts are more inclined to enforce agreements for tangible items such as payments of expenses or rights to property. A promise of housekeeping services or emotional support for a partner may be sincere, but it is much more amorphous than a promise to pay half the phone bill or share the proceeds of a condominium sale.

LIVING TOGETHER

Bob and Carol dated for four months and then decided they wanted to live together without getting married. They both planned to continue their jobs—Bob as a salesperson at a department store and Carol as a junior high school teacher. They decided to formalize their relationship and responsibilities in writing. Carol and Bob prepared a two-page statement that they both signed. In it, they agreed to share equally in living expenses—rent for a new apartment they'll obtain together, electricity, gas, groceries, and telephone (each pays for his or her own long-distance calls). They each will be responsible for their own personal expenses, such as clothes and car payments. If Bob and Carol break up one year later and one of them has not paid half the expenses, the promise to pay half the expenses could be legally enforceable because the agreement was in writing and pertained to identifiable living expenses.

HEALTH CARE POWER OF ATTORNEY

People living together may be concerned about who will have the power to make decisions about their health care in the event that they are unable to make such decisions themselves. For example, if you're unconscious from an accident or from the final stage of a terminal illness, who is authorized to make health care decisions for you?

If you want to designate the person you're living with to make health care decisions, prepare and sign a **power of attorney for health care.** (In the absence of a power of attorney, health care decisions would probably be left to your relatives, such as a mother, father, brother, sister, or adult child.) By signing the form, you designate the individual who is authorized to make decisions about the use or discontinuation of health care. The form also may place limits on the decisions that may be made by the person who has the power of attorney for health care.

The holder of the power of attorney is usually entitled to have access to the patient and to the patient's medical records. The person with power of attorney for health care, however, is not obligated to pay the patient's medical bills.

Ted and Alice met at a dance where Ted was a member of the band and Alice was a guest. After dating two days, Alice moved in with Ted. Alice quit her part-time job as a secretary. Ted continued to work with his successful band. In a romantic moment at 3:00 A.M. two months into the relationship, Ted said, "This is great! I'll take care of you, Alice. I hope we'll always be together!" But four months later, Ted finds a woman with whom he would rather be, and he asks Alice to move out. Alice sues for support and for half of Ted's earnings during the relationship. Alice is likely to lose because the agreement was not specific enough. She apparently did not specifically agree to give up something to obtain particular benefits from Ted. In addition, companionship (and sex) are not bases for an enforceable agreement between two people living together.

If you name someone to have power of attorney for your health care, inform the person who has been named and discuss the circumstances under which life support should be continued or stopped. This will make it easier for the person with power of attorney to make an appropriate decision should the need arise.

WILLS

People who are living together in a committed relationship may wish to draw up wills naming their partners as beneficiaries, at least for certain items. If, for example, the couple acquired property for their mutual use, such as furniture and appliances, each member of the couple may wish to leave their interest in the property to the other in the event of death. In the absence of a will making such a bequest, the property of one member of the couple most likely would pass to blood relatives of the deceased.

When preparing a will, you also may wish to consider leaving other types of property to your partner, such as belongings of a sentimental value or cash.

If you have doubts about the duration of the relationship but want to leave something to your partner upon death if you are still together, the bequest might be made contingent on the partners living together at the time of death. If the parties are living together at the time of death, the will would make the bequest. If the (former) partners are not living together, the bequest would not be made, or perhaps an alternate bequest would be given.

If you and your partner hold property such as a house, condominium, or car in **joint tenancy with right of survivorship**, a will would not be necessary to pass that property to your partner. Property held in such tenancy will pass automatically to the surviving joint tenant. For houses, condominiums, or other real estate, the deed to the property would indicate how tenancy is held. For automobiles, the title would indicate if there are one or more owners. If there is more than one owner, ownership of the car usually would pass to the survivor or survivors upon the death of one of the people listed on the title.

Another issue to consider when drafting a will is who is responsible for making funeral arrangements. If two people who are living together want to designate each other as responsible for preparing funeral arrangements, they should say so in their wills. Otherwise, the responsibility and right of making funeral arrangements probably would fall to a blood relative. Payment of funeral expenses generally comes from the **estate** (the money and property) of the person who died, assuming the person left enough money or property to pay for the funeral.

In addition to specifying responsibility for funeral arrangements in a regular will, you also may wish to specify responsibility for funeral arrangements in a **living will**. A living will is a document in which you leave instructions regarding when life support should be discontinued in the event you are incapacitated and cannot express your desires. For example, in a living will you might direct that you do not want artificial life support, such as a respirator or feeding tube, in the event of irreversible coma or the final stage of a terminal illness.

Since living wills are designed to be read before the time of death, they can be a useful place to express your wishes about funeral arrangements, thus increasing the likelihood that the wishes will be followed. Sometimes regular wills are not read until after the funeral.

If you do not want to sign a living will but want to increase the likelihood that funeral instructions in a regular will are followed, tell your partner, family, and close friends of the location of the will and the presence of funeral instructions in it.

CHAPTER TWO

■

Premarital and
Postmarital Agreements

A PREMARITAL AGREEMENT—also referred to as an **ante-nuptial** or **prenuptial agreement**—is a contract entered into by a man and woman before they marry. The agreement usually describes what each party's rights will be if they divorce or if one of them dies. Premarital agreements most commonly deal with issues of property and financial support for one or both spouses, describing the property and support (if any) to which each party will be entitled in the event of divorce or death. Premarital agreements are not binding regarding custody of children or child support. Regardless of what the parties agree before (or during) the marriage, courts have the power to decide custody and child support according to the best interest of the child.

REASONS FOR PREMARITAL AGREEMENTS

People intending to marry use premarital agreements for several reasons, some of which may be interrelated. Premarital agreements help clarify the parties' expectations and rights for the future. The agreements may avoid uncertainties and fears about how a divorce court might divide property and decide spousal support if the marriage fails.

A man or woman who wants a future spouse to enter into a premarital agreement often has something he or she wants to protect, usually money. One or both partners may want to avoid the risk of a major loss of assets, income, or a family business in the event of a divorce. People marrying for a second or third time might want to make sure that certain assets or personal belongings are passed on to the children or grandchildren of prior marriages rather than to a current spouse.

The less wealthy spouse is generally giving something up by signing a premarital agreement. That spouse (as well as the other spouse) is agreeing to have his or her property rights determined by the agreement rather than by the usual rules of law that a court would apply on divorce or death. As will be discussed later (see chapter 9), courts have rules for dividing property when a couple divorces. In some states (such as California) courts automatically divide equally the property acquired by the husband and wife during the marriage. In most states, courts divide property as the court considers fair, and the result is less predictable. The split could be fifty-fifty or something else.

If one spouse dies, courts normally follow the instructions of that person's will, but the surviving spouse usually is entitled to one third to one half of the estate, regardless of what the deceased spouse's will says. If the husband and wife have signed a valid premarital agreement, however, that agreement will supersede the usual laws for dividing property and income upon death. In many cases, the less wealthy spouse will receive less under the premarital agreement than he or she would receive under the usual laws of divorce or wills.

If the less wealthy spouse will receive less under the agreement than under the general laws of divorce and death, why does he or she choose to sign the agreement? The answer to that question depends on the individual.

Some people prefer to control their fiscal relationship rather than to leave it to state regulation. They may want to avoid uncertainty about what a court might decide if the marriage ends in divorce. For some, the answer may be "love conquers all"—the less wealthy person may just want to marry the other person and not care much about the financial details. For others, the agreement may provide ample security, even if it is not as generous as a judge might be. Still others may not like the agreement, but they are willing to take their chances and hope the relationship and the financial arrangements work out for the best.

CRITERIA FOR A VALID AGREEMENT

The laws governing the validity of premarital agreements vary from state to state. In general, the agreements must be in writing and signed by the parties.

In most states, the parties (particularly the wealthier party) must disclose their income and assets to the other party. This way, the parties will know more about what they might be giving up. In some states, it may be possible to waive a full disclosure of income and assets, but the person waiving that right should do so knowingly, and it is best if each party has at least a general idea of the other's net worth.

Sometimes it is difficult to make a precise statement of a party's net worth. If, for example, the husband or wife owns a business that is **closely held** (meaning shares of the company's stock are not traded on a public stock market), it may be difficult to ascertain the value of the business. In that circumstance, it is usually best to acknowledge the difficulty of precise valuation in the agreement and then state the minimum net worth or the range of possible net worth of the party.

In order to be valid, an agreement must not be the result of **fraud** or **duress**. An agreement is likely to be invalid on the basis of fraud if one person (particularly the wealthier one) deliberately misstates his or her financial condition. For example, if a man hides assets from his future wife so that she will agree to a low level of support in case of divorce, a court probably would declare the agreement invalid. Similarly, if one person exerts excessive emotional pressure on the other to sign the agreement, a court might declare the agreement to be invalid because of duress.

In order to avoid an appearance of duress and to give the parties ample time to consider the agreement, the agreement should be reviewed and signed well before the wedding. Most states do not set a specific time at which premarital agreements must be signed, but the greater amount of time the parties have to consider the agreement, the greater the likelihood a court would find the agreement to be voluntary. For example, if the wealthier person presents the agreement to the prospective spouse for the first time one day before the wedding, a court may later find that the agreement was invalid because of duress. A last-minute premarital agreement is not automatically invalid, but timing may be a significant factor in determining whether the agreement is valid.

WHEN AN AGREEMENT IS ENFORCEABLE

Mary and John, both in their late forties, plan to marry in five months. Each has been married before. Before getting married, however, they wish to clarify their financial relationship. Mary has assets of about $400,000; John has assets of about $200,000. They both work, are capable of self-support, and wish to protect the assets that they will bring into the marriage.

After disclosing their assets to each other and consulting with their individual attorneys, they sign an agreement that provides:

1. Their future earnings will remain their respective separate property as long as the earnings are kept in accounts bearing only the name of the person who earned the money;
2. The savings, investments, and retirement accounts that they bring into the marriage, along with any growth in those assets, will remain separate property after the marriage as long as the assets are held in the name of only one of the parties;
3. Each party waives any right to future alimony or inheritance, although either party is free to include the other in his or her will;
4. The parties, if they wish, may make joint investments, such as in a house, condominium, or car, in which case, title will be held jointly with a **right of survivorship** (which means if one of them dies, the other will receive the property that was jointly held); and
5. They will share payment of common expenses, including housing, utilities, and food, in proportion to their incomes.

Since the agreement appears to be fair and not made under duress, it is likely to be valid and enforceable.

An agreement might be valid even if both parties were not represented by lawyers, but using lawyers helps ensure that the agreement is drafted properly and that both parties are making informed decisions.

The lawyer for the wealthier party usually prepares the initial draft of the agreement. The less wealthy party and that party's attorney, if there is one, should review the agreement carefully and ask questions about any matters that are uncertain. The likelihood of having a valid, enforceable agreement increases if the less wealthy party's interests are well represented and some back-and-forth negotiations take place.

In order to demonstrate that the parties truly know what they are agreeing to, some attorneys favor taking additional steps to illustrate the knowledge of each party about the agreement. In addition to signing the agreement, the parties also may place their initials on pages with key provisions, such as the provisions of the agreement pertaining to disclosures of assets, distribution of property, and support.

The parties, particularly the less wealthy party, might be asked to prepare a handwritten statement, in their own words, reflecting an understanding of and consent to the agreement. Alternatively, the signing of the agreement might be videotaped (or audiotaped) with the parties providing oral statements of their understanding and consent to the agreement (in addition to their written consent).

AMOUNT OF SUPPORT

State laws do not set a specific amount of support that must be provided in premarital agreements.

If, after a divorce, the parties are capable of self-support, based on their assets, income, and job skills, a court probably would uphold an agreement that provided no property or support to the less wealthy spouse.

If, on the other hand, the less wealthy spouse cannot be self-sufficient and the agreement provides little or no property or support, courts in most states are likely to step in and order some distribution of property or support in favor of the less wealthy spouse. That amount will vary from state to state. In some states, the amount needs to reach only a subsistence level—enough to keep the less wealthy spouse off the welfare rolls. Many courts will apply broader notions of fairness and require support at a level higher than subsistence, particularly after a long-term marriage.

A standard used by some courts is **unconscionability**. Unconscionability refers to agreements which are unusually harsh and unfair. Some courts define an unconscionable agreement as one that no sensible person would offer and no sensible person, not under duress or delusion, would accept. Since the standard of unconscionability is subjective, courts have interpreted the term in different ways, but if a court finds an agreement to be unconscionable, the agreement will not be enforced. For discussion of the general standards for dividing property and alimony/maintenance in the absence of a valid premarital agreement, see chapters 9 and 10.

To promote fairness and avoid unconscionability, many lawyers drafting premarital agreements favor including an **escalator clause** or a **phase-in provision** that will increase the amount of assets or support given to the less wealthy spouse based on the length of the marriage or an increase in the wealthier party's assets or income after the agreement is made.

If the wealthier party is concerned that his or her assets could drop sharply at a later time, the wealthier spouse may wish to include a provision to provide protection in such a circumstance. If the agreement provides for a fixed dollar amount to the less wealthy spouse, the wealthier party might add a provision that says in no event shall the amount of property given to the other spouse exceed half (or some other percentage) of the wealthier party's assets. Alternatively, the payment of assets at time of divorce (or death) could be set as a percentage of the wealthier party's assets at the time of divorce (or death).

NONBINDING ISSUES

Although premarital agreements can be binding on issues of division of property and alimony, they are not binding on issues of child custody. In other words, parties cannot agree in advance of the birth of a child how custody of the child will be decided in the event of divorce. Courts remain the ultimate guardian of a child's best interest, and courts do not want to encourage a husband and wife to bargain away what is best for the child. A court may consider what the parties declared to be best for the child in a premarital agreement, but the court will not be bound by an agreement entered into before marriage.

A premarital agreement on child support also is not binding on the court for similar reasons. If the agreement on child support meets the child's reasonable needs, the court may choose to follow it, but it is not required to do so. For description of the standards for child custody and child support, see chapters 11 and 12.

RELATED DOCUMENTS

At the time the parties sign a premarital agreement, they also may sign related documents to help carry out their wishes. For example, the man and woman may enter into a **contract to make a will,** by which they agree in advance about what the terms of their wills will be. The parties may wish to agree that children from prior marriages (or the current marriage) will receive a specified amount of their estates.

Contracts to make a will have the advantage of clarifying the parties' rights and responsibilities, but such contracts carry the disadvantage of loss of flexibility. If circumstances change, a party who signed the contract to make a will may not be able to change his or her will unless both parties consent. If, for instance, one party wishes to include a new person or charity in the will, that party may no longer be able to do so, depending on how the contract was written.

Another document that may be signed at the time of a premarital agreement is a document to create a **trust.** A trust is a legal device by which the title to property is held by one party for the benefit of another party. For example, money in a bank account, shares of stock in a company, or deeds to land may be placed in a trust. A **trustee** will have the power to manage the property in the trust for benefit of the person for whom the trust was created (the **beneficiary**).

A trust created in connection with a premarital agreement might be used to manage and protect the assets of the wealthier party. A trust also might be used to establish a fund for the benefit of the less wealthy party. In some premarital agreements, the wealthier party may agree to place a certain amount of money each year into a trust for the benefit of the less wealthy party. The deposits would continue to be made for as long as the marriage lasts (perhaps up to a maximum number of years or a maximum dollar amount). In the event of divorce or death, the less wealthy party's entitlement to assets might be limited to whatever was in the trust.

POSTMARITAL AGREEMENTS

Postmarital agreements or **postnuptial agreements** are agreements entered into after a marriage has taken place but before the parties seek to end their marriage. As with premarital agreements, one or both of the parties is usually seeking to protect assets or income in the event of divorce or death.

A married couple may seek to enter into a postmarital agreement after a significant financial change or a period of marital conflict.

The law regarding the validity and enforcement of postmarital agreements is not well developed.

The standard for enforcement of postmarital agreements most likely is similar to the standards discussed earlier for enforcement of premarital agreements. Key criteria for validity of the agreements include: full disclosure of assets, absence of duress, and fairness.

When a man and woman are married (instead of just contemplating marriage), they may be held to a very high standard of fairness when dealing with each other on financial issues—perhaps a higher standard than would be the case if they were entering into a premarital agreement.

When entering into a postmarital agreement, it would be a good idea for the parties to articulate in writing why they are entering into the agreement and to be sure the agreement is fair for both parties.

■

CHAPTER THREE

Valid and Invalid Marriages

MOST STATES DEFINE MARRIAGE as a civil contract between a man and woman to become husband and wife. The moment a man and woman marry, their relationship acquires a legal status. The rights and obligations of married persons are not the same as single persons. Married persons may have rights to their partner's property and future income; they may be responsible for each other's debts; and they are subject to different tax rates than single persons. State and federal laws determine the scope of the married person's new rights and duties.

REQUIREMENTS FOR GETTING MARRIED

The requirements for getting married are simple, although they vary from state to state. In general, a man and woman wishing to marry must obtain a license in the state in which they wish to be married, usually from a county clerk or a clerk of court. The fee usually is low.

Many states require the man and woman to have blood tests for venereal disease—but not for HIV, the virus that causes AIDS—before the license is issued. Some states do not require this test if the two already have been living together. If the test shows that a would-be spouse has a venereal disease, certain states will not issue a license. Other states will allow the marriage as long as the couple knows the disease is present.

In some states, the couple must show proof of immunity or vaccination for certain diseases. A few states demand a general physical examination. The local marriage license bureau or clerk of court will be able to tell you what is necessary to obtain a marriage license.

If one or both of the parties have been married before, the earlier marriage must have been ended by death, divorce, or annulment (although in some states, if a marriage was never valid, a legal action for annulment may not be necessary).

Parties who wish to marry must have the **capacity** to do so. That means the man and woman must understand that they are being married and what it means to be married. If because of drunkenness, mental illness, severe mental retardation, or some other problem, one of the parties lacks capacity, the marriage will not be valid.

Close blood relatives cannot marry, although in some states, first cousins can marry. Of the states that allow first cousins to marry, a few also require that one of the cousins no longer be able to conceive children.

Most, but not all, states require a waiting period, generally one to five days, between the time the license is issued and the time of the marriage ceremony. The purpose of the waiting period is to give a brief cooling-off time during which the parties can change their minds if they wish. The waiting period can be waived for good reason. For example, if the groom is arriving in the bride's town only one day before the wedding, but the state has a three-day waiting period, the waiting period can probably be waived by a judge or clerk of court.

In most states, a man or woman may marry at age eighteen without parental consent. Most states also allow persons age sixteen and seventeen to marry with consent of their parents or a judge.

A marriage that is valid in the state or country where it was performed generally will be considered valid in a state or country to which the couple later moves, unless the state or country to which the couple moved has a very strong policy against such marriages.

THE MARRIAGE CEREMONY

A marriage ceremony may be religious or civil.

A religious ceremony should be conducted under the customs of the religion, or, in the case of Native Americans, under the customs of the tribe. Religious ceremonies normally are conducted by religious officials, such as ministers, priests, or rabbis. Native American ceremonies may be presided over by a tribal chief or other designated official.

Civil ceremonies, on the other hand, are usually conducted by judges. In some states, county clerks or other government officials also may conduct civil ceremonies, but contrary to some popular legends, no state authorizes ship captains to perform marriages.

Most states require one or two witnesses to sign the marriage certificate. The person who performs the marriage ceremony has a duty to send a copy of the marriage certificate to the county or state agency that records marriage certificates. Failure to send the marriage certificate to the appropriate agency does not necessarily nullify the marriage, but it may make proof of the marriage more difficult.

States generally do not require that certain words be used in a marriage ceremony, but the person or persons conducting the ceremony should indicate that the man and woman agree to be married.

Most states consider a couple to be married when the ceremony ends. Lack of subsequent sexual relations does not automatically affect the validity of the marriage, although in some states nonconsummation could be a basis for having the marriage annulled. (For more information on annulments, see pages 65 to 66.)

CHANGE OF NAME

A woman who marries may change her last name (also known as "surname") to that of her husband, but she is not legally required to do so. In the past, it was widely assumed that a woman would change her last name to her husband's name when she married. Now society recognizes a woman's right to take her husband's name, keep her original name, or use both names. The general rule is that if a woman uses a certain name consistently and honestly, then that is her true name.

COMMON-LAW MARRIAGES

In times past, particularly the frontier days, it was common for states to consider a woman and man to be married if they lived together for a certain length of time, had sexual intercourse, and held themselves out as husband and wife, even though they never went through a marriage ceremony. Such a marriage was often called a **common-law marriage**.

Today, at least three quarters of the states no longer recognize common-law marriages. The remaining states recognize common-law marriages, but with significant restrictions. In order for there to be a legal common-law marriage (in the states that recognize them), the couple must: have the capacity to marry; regard themselves as husband and wife; live together; and clearly represent themselves to others as being husband and wife. Merely living together is not enough to create a marriage.

If a common-law marriage is valid, the partners have the same rights and duties as if there had been a ceremonial marriage. An interesting problem occurs if a couple had a valid common-law marriage in a state that recognizes common-law marriages, but then moved to a state that does not recognize common-law marriages. Would the marriage still be valid? Under principles of **conflict of laws**, the answer usually would be "yes." Conflict of laws principles generally state that if a contract (in this case a marriage agreement) is valid in the place in which it was created, it will be treated as valid in a state to which the parties move, even though the parties could not have entered into such an agreement in the new state.

A legal common-law marriage may end only with a formal divorce. There is not a United States counterpart to the tradition in Muslim law that allows a divorce to be accomplished by one party to the marriage—in Muslim law, that's the husband—pronouncing the Talek: "I divorce thee. I divorce thee. I divorce thee."

INVALID MARRIAGES

Occasionally, people who live as a married couple learn that their marriage is not legal. For example, one supposed spouse may have kept a prior marriage secret, or both may have thought incorrectly that an earlier marriage had ended in divorce or the death of a spouse. Or a marriage may be invalid because it is between close relatives, underage persons, or people incapable of entering into the marriage contract because of mental incompetence.

If a marriage was improper for reasons such as these, a court may grant an **annulment** instead of a divorce. An annulment is a legal declaration that a valid marriage never existed. An annulment is different from a divorce in that a divorce is a legal declaration that a *valid* marriage is over. Sometimes people want an annulment because their marriage was of short duration or because they feel they got married for the wrong reasons. Such circumstances, by themselves, are not a proper basis for an annulment. Instead, the couple must obtain a divorce to end their marriage. (Divorces will be discussed more on pages 66 to 70.)

When a court grants an annulment, the parties often are free to go their separate ways without any further obligations to each other. Many states, however, apply additional principles of law to protect a person who thought he or she was in a valid marriage but, in fact, was not. An individual who believed that he or she was in a valid marriage but was not is referred to as the **putative spouse**, and the rule of law that gives that person protection is sometimes referred to as the **putative-spouse doctrine**. (In some states, protection also may be given without labeling the remedy the "putative-spouse doctrine.")

Under the putative-spouse doctrine, a putative spouse may be entitled to the same benefits and rights of a legal spouse for as long as she or he reasonably believed the marriage to be valid. From time to time, people discover that their marriage is invalid only when filing for divorce. After a long union that both parties believed to be valid, a court may refuse to declare the marriage invalid and require a divorce to end the marriage. In that event, the usual rules of property distribution and support apply. (Later chapters cover these topics.)

If one party to the marriage thought the marriage was valid, but the other party knew the marriage was not, an additional principle may apply: **estoppel**. Estoppel means that a person's conduct may prevent that person from doing something he or she would otherwise be entitled to do. For example, if one party to a marriage tricked the other into thinking the marriage was valid, a court might not allow the deceiver to declare the marriage invalid. Thus, the deceiving partner would not be able to use deception to profit from property division or support.

If the party who was deceived learned recently of the deception and wanted to get out of the marriage using an annulment instead of divorce, the court probably would allow the annulment. On the other hand, if the party who was deceived learned of the deception and chose to continue in the marriage for a long period of time before seeking to end the marriage, the doctrine of **laches** (long delay) may prevent even the "innocent" party from seeking to declare the marriage invalid. In that case, the parties may be required to follow the rules of divorce rather than annulment.

SAME-SEX MARRIAGES

As of 1996, no state has passed a law recognizing marriages of persons of the same sex. If two members of the same sex were to go through a marriage ceremony, the courts would not consider the marriage to be valid, and, in the event the parties split up, they could not seek a legal divorce.

Periodically, there are proposals before state legislatures to allow homosexual marriages, but so far none has become law. In 1993, however, the Hawaii Supreme Court ruled that denying same-sex couples the right to marry might violate the equal protection provisions of Hawaii's state constitution. The case is still under consideration in the Hawaii courts.

DOMESTIC PARTNERSHIPS

Some governmental units (mostly cities so far) have passed laws providing for **domestic partnerships**. Domestic partnerships can be used by homosexual couples and by heterosexual couples who are living together without being married. To become domestic partners, the couple usually must register their relationship at a government office and declare that they are in a "committed" relationship.

Domestic partnerships provide some—but not all—of the legal benefits of marriage. Some of the common benefits are:

1. the right to coverage on a family health insurance policy
2. the right to family leave to take care of a sick partner (to the same extent a person would be able to use family leave to care for a sick spouse)
3. bereavement leave
4. visiting rights to hospitals and jails
5. rent control benefits (to the same extent a spouse would retain reduced rent if his or her partner died).

Domestic partnership laws are not uniform. The level of benefits varies with the jurisdiction that enacted the laws.

Even without domestic partnership laws, some insurance companies will offer family rates on health and auto policies to unmarried couples who demonstrate a long-term, financially interdependent relationship.

CHAPTER FOUR

■

Financial Aspects
of Marriage

MOST PROPERTY THAT IS ACQUIRED DURING THE MARRIAGE is considered marital, or community, property. For example, wages earned by the husband and wife during marriage generally are considered marital property. If one or both spouses buy a house or establish a business during the marriage, that usually will be marital property, particularly if the house or business is purchased with the husband's and wife's earnings.

Separate property is property that each spouse owned before the marriage. Separate property also includes inheritances and gifts (except perhaps gifts between spouses) acquired during marriage. During and after the marriage, each spouse may keep control of his or her separate property. Each spouse may buy, sell, and borrow money on his or her separate property. Income earned from separate property, such as interest, dividends, or rent, generally is classified as separate property. However, in some states that recognize community property, these profits may become marital property.

Separate property can become marital property if it is mixed with marital property. If, for example, a wife owned an apartment building before the marriage and she deposited rent checks into a joint checking account, the rent money probably would become marital property, although the building is likely to remain the wife's separate property as long as she kept it in her name. If the wife changed the title on the building from her name alone to the names of both herself and her husband, that probably would convert the building into marital property. In addition, if one spouse put a great deal of work into the other spouse's separate property, that could convert the separate property into marital property, or it could give the spouse who contributed the work a right to some form of payback. Chapter 9 will discuss how courts divide marital property in a divorce.

A husband and wife may own property together during the marriage. This occurs automatically in **community property states**. Nine states—Arizona, California, Idaho, Louisiana, Nevada, New Mexico, Texas, Washington, and Wisconsin, as well as Puerto Rico—use the community property system. These jurisdictions hold that each spouse owns equally the income earned and property acquired during a marriage. This is true even if one spouse supplied all the income. In the other states, spouses generally own property under one of the following three forms of co-ownership:

- **Joint tenancy.** A form of ownership that exists when two or more people own property that includes a **right of survivorship**. Each person has the right to possess the property. If one partner dies, the survivor becomes the sole owner. Any two people—not just spouses—may own property as joint tenants. A creditor may claim the debtor's interest in joint tenancy property.

- **Tenancy by the entirety.** Allowed only in some states, tenancy by the entirety is a type of co-ownership of property by a husband and wife. Like joint tenancy, it includes a right of survivorship. But a creditor of one spouse may not **attach** (seize) the property. Each party usually must consent to the sale of the property. Divorce may result in a division of the property.

- **Tenancy in common.** This form of co-ownership gives each person control over his or her share of the property, and the shares need not be equal. The law does not limit tenancy in common to spouses. A tenancy in common has no right of survivorship; when one spouse dies, his or her share passes to the heirs, either by will or by state laws.

Tenancy rules vary from one state to another. Some tenancies are complex and must be created in a precise manner; otherwise the courts may not enforce them.

DEBTS

Husbands and wives may be responsible for debts incurred by the other depending on the nature of the debt as well as where the couple resides. If both husband and wife have co-signed for the debt, both will be responsible for paying it. For instance, assume the husband and wife apply together for a charge card. If both sign the application form and promise to pay the charge bills, both will be responsible for paying off the balance to the credit card company or store, even if only one of them made the purchases and the other disapproved. Similarly, if a husband and wife co-sign on a mortgage for a home, both of them are potentially liable to the mortgage company, even if one of them no longer lives in the home. In community property states, a husband and wife may likewise be responsible for debts incurred by the other.

A husband and wife can also be responsible for each other's debts, even if they have not co-signed, if the debt is considered a **family expense**. Some states have **family expense statutes** that make a husband or wife liable for expenses incurred for the benefit of the family, even if he or she did not sign for or approve of the expense in advance. Still other states impose the family expense obligation by common law without a statute. Thus, if the wife charged groceries at a local store or took the couple's child to a doctor for care, the husband could be liable because these are expenses for the benefit of the family.

On the other hand, if the wife runs up bills for a personal holiday or the husband buys expensive coins for his coin collection, the other spouse normally would not be liable unless he or she co-signed for the debt. But again, in community property states, a husband or wife generally is liable for the debts of the other.

Each spouse, however, generally is not liable for debts the other spouse brought into the marriage. Such debts belong to the spouse who incurred them.

In many states, however, a debt incurred before marriage (including a child support debt) could be collected against marital property of a new marriage. Thus, for example, if a man was $15,000 behind in support to children of a first marriage, but the man owned a house or bank account in joint tenancy with his second wife, those assets might be taken by a court to pay off the old debt. If the second wife is worried about the first wife or other creditors from the first marriage placing a claim on assets of the second marriage, the second wife should keep most of her property in her own name rather than in joint tenancy with her husband.

If one spouse owns a business and the other does not, the spouse who does not own the business normally would not be liable for business debts unless the nonowner co-signed on the debt or the couple resided in a community property state.

It is common for institutions that lend money to small businesses to want personal guarantees of payment from the owner of the business, and not just from the business itself. In the event the debt is not paid, lenders would like as many pockets to reach into as a possible. If the owner of the business owns a home, the lender may want to use the home as collateral for the business loan. That means that the spouse of the business owner, along with the business owner, may be asked to sign a paper allowing use of the home as collateral. Thus, the home could be lost if the business cannot pay off its debts.

Wives and husbands are entitled to open credit accounts in their individual names, and creditors cannot require a spouse to co-sign on an account unless the party seeking credit lives in a community property state. In that case both signatures can be required, since spouses are liable for each other's debts incurred during the marriage.

TAXES

If the husband's and wife's names and signatures appear on a state or federal personal income tax return, both are liable for the taxes. If a couple files jointly, the Internal Revenue Service generally holds each spouse responsible for the entire debt.

In some circumstances, a spouse who signed a joint tax return can be excused from liability if the spouse can prove that he or she is an **innocent spouse**. A wife or husband can be considered an innocent spouse if he or she did not know—and had no reason to know—that the tax return understated the true tax.

That is often hard to prove. For example, the *Wall Street Journal* reported a case in which the wife of an IRS auditor did not know that her husband was taking bribes, but neither did she ask how they could afford expensive education for their children and country club dues on his government salary. The wife, as well as the husband, was found liable for $150,000 in unpaid taxes and penalties. (The husband also went to jail.)

On the other hand, a wife who relied on her husband and a certified public accountant to file a proper tax return was held not to be liable when a deduction for one of the husband's tax shelters was not allowed by the IRS.

If a married person wants full protection against possible liability for inaccurate tax returns filed by his or her spouse, the best approach is to file as "married filing separate return." That, however, usually results in a higher combined tax payment for the husband and wife than if they filed a joint return.

Depending on the income levels of each spouse, a married couple's income tax payments may be higher or lower than the taxes would be if the couple remained single. If one spouse has a high taxable income and the other spouse has a relatively low taxable income, they will generally pay less income tax if they are married and filing a joint return than if they are single and filing as single persons.

For wives and husbands who both have high incomes, their combined tax will be higher when they file as married persons than if they file as two single persons. Members of Congress periodically promise to remove the "marriage penalty" from federal income tax laws, but as of early 1996, that has not happened.

Years ago, there were stories about financially well-off married couples who would travel to the Caribbean each December, obtain a divorce, file tax returns as single persons for that year to save money, and then remarry in the new year. Such a practice could be regarded as tax fraud. In any case, the savings are not as great as they were in years past.

DOING BUSINESS TOGETHER

Wives and husbands, of course, can do business together. They can be business partners, just as any other two people, whether related or not. They could set up a corporation and both be owners and employees of the corporation; they could form a partnership; or one could own the business and employ the other. Wages and benefits, including health insurance and retirement plans, can be paid, just as they would for any other employee.

If wages and benefits are being paid to a spouse or child, the amount usually should not be more than what is reasonable or fair market value. If artificially high payments are made, the business could get into trouble with the Internal Revenue Service.

GIFTS BETWEEN SPOUSES

One spouse may make gifts to the other spouse in any amount without paying federal gift taxes if the spouse receiving the gift is a U.S. resident. However, it must be an outright gift or set up as a proper trust. Most, but not all, state laws have done away with state taxes on gifts between spouses.

The same is not true, however, with respect to gifts to other family members or to persons outside the family. Gifts to children, other relatives, people outside the family, and trusts may be taxable if they exceed a certain amount per year. As of 1996, under federal tax law, one person may give someone other than a spouse up to $10,000 per year without paying any tax on the gift. A married couple could give $20,000 to a person each year without paying a gift tax. Both single people and married couples can make an unlimited number of such tax-free gifts each year. However, if some or all of the gifts are made above the allowable dollar amounts, the overage will be deducted from the $600,000 federal estate tax credit that all Americans have. So if the annual gifts exceeded the permissible amount by $30,000, then the gift maker would have only a $570,000 credit, and his or her estate would be liable for taxes on that $30,000 if the estate exceeded $570,000.

■

CHAPTER FIVE

Having Children

THE UNITED STATES SUPREME COURT HAS DECLARED that the decision of whether or not to have a child is a very personal one and that the decision is protected by the right of privacy or liberty interest under the United States Constitution. This means that individuals who wish to have a child cannot be barred from doing so (unless perhaps they are incarcerated). In addition, individuals who do not wish to have a child have a legal right to obtain and use contraceptives.

One spouse cannot legally force the other spouse to have a child. Conversely, if a woman becomes pregnant, neither her partner nor the courts can force her to have an abortion. The decision of whether to continue a pregnancy belongs to the woman.

If a husband or wife wants to have a child, but their partner does not, that could be a basis for a divorce. A disagreement on such a fundamental issue could be an "irreconcilable difference" under the no-fault divorce laws of most states. In states that have grounds for divorce based on someone being at fault, a disagreement on the question of whether to have children might be viewed as "mental cruelty," and thus a basis for ending the marriage.

MEDICALLY ASSISTED PREGNANCIES

Medical science now offers individuals who wish to become parents a variety of medically assisted means, including artificial insemination and in vitro fertilization. These medical procedures have legal implications that vary by state. Generally, however, if both husband

and wife consent to artificial insemination or in vitro fertilization, the rights and duties of the husband, wife, and child will be the same as if the child had been naturally conceived.

SURROGATE PARENTHOOD

In a **surrogate parenting arrangement**, a woman agrees, with or without payment, to bear a child for another couple. This usually occurs when the wife cannot conceive or carry a child to term. In most surrogate parenting arrangements, the husband's sperm, through artificial insemination, fertilizes an egg belonging to either the wife or the surrogate mother. This makes the husband the biological father of the child in either case.

The surrogate mother agrees to give up all parental rights at birth. Then the wife of the biological father legally adopts the child. A few states outlaw this arrangement when the surrogate mother receives payment. Other states have laws that restrict surrogate parenting arrangements or that might give the surrogate mother the right to keep the child after birth. Anyone thinking about entering into a surrogate parenting arrangement should seek legal advice first.

ABORTION

Women in America still have a right to an abortion, and it appears that will remain the law in the United States for many years to come. In the 1992 case of *Planned Parenthood* v. *Casey,* the U.S. Supreme Court reaffirmed its 1973 decision in *Roe* v. *Wade* that women have a constitutional right to seek an abortion before the fetus is viable outside the womb. The Court also ruled that states may not require a woman to notify her husband before she seeks an abortion. (The Court was particularly concerned about the impact of a notification requirement on women who are in an abusive relationship.)

While it affirmed a woman's right to seek an abortion early in pregnancy, the Supreme Court in *Casey* also held that states may regulate many other aspects of abortion. After a fetus is viable, it is permissible for states to prohibit abortions unless the mother's life or health is endangered.

PUBLIC FUNDING FOR ABORTION

States that voluntarily fund abortions for low-income women

States that are under court order to fund abortions for low-income women on the same terms as other pregnancy-related conditions and general health services

States with pending lawsuits challenging public funding bans as violations of state constitutional protections

States both under court order and with pending lawsuits

States in white have restrictive funding policies

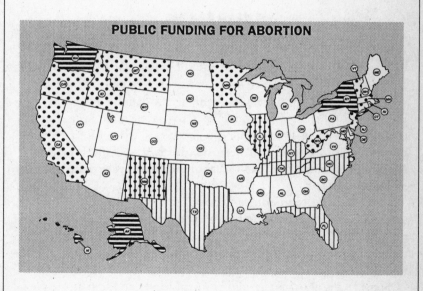

PUBLIC FUNDING FOR ABORTION

Fact Sheet on Public Funding for Abortion (1996) published by the Reproductive Freedom Project of the American Civil Liberties Union.

States also may impose a waiting period to obtain an abortion (unless the mother's health is endangered). In *Casey,* the Court upheld Pennsylvania's twenty-four-hour waiting period as a reasonable means of assuring that a woman who seeks an abortion makes a deliberate decision. During that waiting period, states also may require that the providers of abortions inform the women about the risks of abortion and alternatives to abortion.

A statute requiring parental consent before a minor could seek an abortion also was upheld, although the statute also allowed a minor to forego asking parents and seek permission from a judge instead if the facts of the case supported bypass of parental consent.

The scope of regulation and funding of abortions by the government varies from state to state. (See the map on page 35.)

CHILDBIRTH

Parents generally are free to select the place at which their child will be born. They may choose a hospital, their own home, or a birthing center staffed by midwives if such centers are available in their area.

Under federal law a hospital equipped to handle delivering babies may not turn away a woman in active labor even if the woman is uninsured. The law prohibiting hospitals from turning away patients who are in urgent need of care is called the **Emergency Medical Treatment and Active Labor Act**—also referred to as the **anti-dumping law.**

If parents are considering an at-home delivery, they should make sure the mother receives good prenatal care and that the health care provider believes the delivery will not pose significant risks to the mother or child. If the delivery is risky for the mother or child, the mother should deliver at a hospital equipped to handle high-risk cases.

Some states allow nurse-midwives to deliver children at the parents' home or at a birthing center. Other states allow nurse-midwives to practice only at hospitals or under the direct supervision of a physician.

As health care technology improves and as health insurance companies seek to reduce the cost of health care, it is increasingly common for mother and child to remain in the hospital for only a short period of time after delivery—often twenty-four hours or less for a normal vaginal delivery and two or three days for a cesarean section. If the health care provider believes a longer hospital stay is necessary, that usually will be ordered.

If the patient wants a longer stay, but the health care provider or insurance company does not think the additional stay is necessary, the patient probably will have to pay in full for the extra stay. Patients may appeal decisions to deny coverage. The patient's contract with the health insurance company or health maintenance organization (HMO) will specify the details of the appeal system.

It is common, however, for the first appeal to be an informal one—a phone call or letter to the insurance company or HMO. If the informal appeal is not satisfactory to the patient, a more formal appeal usually can be taken, such as a hearing before administrators or physicians who work for the insurance company or HMO. If that also fails, the patient might be entitled (depending on the nature of the contract and the state in which the patient lives) to seek outside relief, such as through the court system or a neutral arbitrator.

Fathers or other family members may wish to be present at the delivery of a child. The decision of whether or not fathers or other family members are allowed in the delivery room normally is left to the hospital's regulation. Most hospitals permit fathers to be present during delivery, although many hospitals prefer that the father and mother have gone through some training before the delivery, such as a Lamaze class. Parents should check with their hospital about other rules and about what persons other than fathers are allowed in the delivery room.

PATERNITY

A man who fathers a child by a woman to whom he is not married generally can acknowledge his **paternity** by signing the child's birth certificate or another document soon after the child's birth.

If a man does not admit that a child is his, a woman can file suit against him to prove that he is the father and to obtain child support. Support for a child born out of wedlock is established using the same support guidelines for a child whose parents are obtaining a divorce. (Child support is discussed in chapter 11.) In many states, fathers of children born out of wedlock also may be obliged to help pay the mother's medical expenses associated with the pregnancy and delivery.

Paternity cases usually involve use of scientific evidence. Blood tests, including DNA testing, can prove to near certainty that a man is or is not the father of the child.

As with a child born to married parents, the obligation of support usually lasts until the child is an adult (depending on the state, the age of adulthood may be between eighteen and twenty-one, with eighteen being the most common). If a father refuses to support his child, a court may garnish his wages, seize his property or bank accounts, and even send him to jail.

RIGHTS AND RESPONSIBILITIES OF PARENTS

Parents have a right to control the care and upbringing of their children. This gives parents the power to make various decisions affecting the child, including where to live, what school to attend, what religion to follow, and what medical treatment to obtain.

Normally the state may not interfere in these decisions. Only in life-threatening or extreme situations will the courts step in to overrule parents. For example, when a child might die without the medical care that the parents refuse to provide, a judge may make the child a ward of the court (or the state) and order that the care be provided. Parents have been prosecuted for withholding medical treatment from seriously ill children. This has occurred even in situations where parents have followed their religious beliefs.

Although children can be hard to control (particularly adolescents), parents have the legal authority to control their children's behavior and social lives. Parents may discipline or punish their children appropriately. They may not, however, use cruel methods or excessive force; that constitutes child abuse.

If a child causes damage to another person or property, the parents may be liable for damages. Some states, for example, have statutes that make parents liable for vandalism caused by their children up to a certain dollar amount, such as $500 or $1,000. If a child is severely out of control, the state may take custody of a child.

If a child has an auto accident while driving a parent's car, the parent's auto insurance policy generally will cover the loss to the same extent it would if the parent had been driving the car (although parents usually have to pay higher insurance premiums to cover young drivers).

Parents are legally responsible for their children until they reach the age of majority (usually eighteen), marry, or leave home to support themselves. In some states, divorced parents may be obliged to pay for a child's college education or trade school. (See pages 114 to 115.) In addition, a parent's duty to support a disabled child might continue for the child's entire life.

NEGLECT AND ABUSE LAWS

Under state laws, it is a criminal offense for parents and legal guardians to fail to meet children's basic needs, including food, clothing, shelter, medical treatment, and supervision. Such failure constitutes **child neglect**.

Child abuse laws make it a crime for adults to abuse children in their care. Such adults include parents, legal guardians, other adults in the home, and baby-sitters. Supervising adults may not go beyond reasonable physical punishment. For example, adults who beat children so severely that the children require medical treatment have violated these laws. Child abuse laws cover not only physical abuse and sexual abuse, but also emotional abuse, such as subjecting a child to extreme public humiliation.

A person may be guilty of child abuse that he or she did not personally commit if that person had legal responsibility for the child and failed to protect the child from the abuser.

The law compels a wide range of people who have contact with children to report suspected child abuse or neglect. Such people include doctors, nurses, teachers, and social workers. A person who is required to report suspected neglect or abuse may face civil or criminal penalties for failure to do so. Relatives and friends who do not have a professional relationship with the child generally do not have a legal duty to report.

States often encourage the reporting of suspected abuse through special hot lines. The laws of most states encourage persons to make reports of abuse by granting them immunity from defamation suits by the accused parents if they make the report in **good faith**— meaning the person who made the report genuinely suspected abuse, even if it later turns out that abuse did not occur.

Some states keep central lists of suspected child abuse cases. This helps identify abusers, such as parents who take their children to different hospitals in order to conceal evidence that they have repeatedly abused their children.

If the state takes a child away from a parent who has abused or neglected the child, the state usually seeks to reunite the family after correction of the problems that led to removal. This, however, is not always possible. If, for example, the parent makes little effort to improve or does not satisfactorily complete parenting skills programs offered by the state, then the state may ask a court to end all parental rights. If this happens, the legal bonds between parents and child are completely and permanently cut. The child then may be adopted by another family.

RIGHTS OF CHILDREN

The law defines children as unmarried persons under the age of majority—usually eighteen—who have not left home to support themselves.

Children have a right to be supported by their parents. As mentioned in the last section, the right of support includes food, shelter, clothing, and medical care. Parents are also obliged to arrange for the education of their children either at school or at home. If parents seek to educate their children at home, the parents usually must prove to the state that they offer a genuine education program at home. Children taught at home may be subject to state testing to ensure that the children are making satisfactory progress in their education.

Children also have a right to be educated by the government through high school (assuming the child is not expelled from school for misconduct). Under federal law, children with significant physical or mental handicaps have a right to government-paid special education programs to meet their needs. If a parent believes a child needs a special education program, but the government is not providing one, the parent can appeal the issue through administrative agencies within the school system and through the courts if necessary.

Mature minors (often defined as children over the age of twelve) are allowed to make their own decisions regarding certain medical procedures, even if parents disagree with the child's choice. For example, in most states parents do not have an absolute veto power over a minor's decision to use contraceptives or obtain an abortion. In many states, minors also can seek treatment for venereal disease without notification or consent of the parents. In addition, in some states, a mature minor can seek and obtain short-term mental health treatment or counseling without parental consent.

If a child receives a large sum of money, such as through inheritance, payment of a damage award for a personal injury, or starring in a television series, the law provides protection regarding how the money is to be managed. The law generally requires the appointment of a **guardian** to manage the child's finances.

The guardian could be a parent or someone other than a parent. Sometimes there will be two guardians—one a parent and the other a non-family member, such as an attorney or a bank officer. Guardians are required to make sure the money is well managed and spent for the child's best interest. The money cannot be used for the primary benefit of other family members. If a guardian spends the money for the guardian's own benefit or in some other way mismanages the funds, the guardian can be personally liable for the amount lost.

To help ensure that the child's money is properly invested and spent, the court may require that the guardian file periodic

accountings with the court, itemizing the child's assets, explaining how the money has been spent, and outlining plans for future expenditures.

The law allows children to sue, including, for example, for personal injuries suffered in an auto accident or a poorly maintained park. In most instances, the child's parent or legal guardian must begin the suit in the child's name.

Children accused of committing crimes are handled by the juvenile courts of their state, not the regular criminal justice system. (In many states, children accused of serious crimes who are above a certain age—sometimes as low as thirteen—may be tried in court as adults.) Juvenile courts entitle children to only some of the procedural safeguards that adults receive, but juvenile courts have more freedom to deal with juveniles in an effort to rehabilitate them. A child on trial as a juvenile, for example, usually does not have a right to a jury trial, but the child generally may not be confined beyond the age of eighteen.

DUTIES OF ADULT CHILDREN
TOWARD THEIR PARENTS

Adult children normally have no legal responsibilities toward their parents. In return, their parents have no legal duties toward them. However, there are exceptions. In some states, children must support parents who otherwise would be on welfare. Children usually can avoid paying support if they can show that the parents did not adequately care for them when they were minors.

In some states, adult children may have to contribute to the support of a parent who is in a state hospital or mental institution. However, the children's ability to pay—not the actual costs of the care—usually determines how much the children must pay.

CHAPTER SIX

■

Adoption

Each year in the united states, there are approximately 105,000 adoptions. Slightly more than half of these are **related adoptions**, meaning the person or persons adopting the child are a blood relation or stepparent of the child. Slightly less than half of the adoptions are **unrelated adoptions**, meaning the person or persons adopting are not related to the child. One type of unrelated adoption involves children born in foreign countries. Between 7,000 and 10,000 children born in foreign countries are adopted by U.S. residents each year.

RELATED ADOPTIONS

Related adoptions are comparatively simple, assuming that no one objects. One of the most common types of adoptions is by a stepfather or stepmother. If the biological parent who the stepfather or stepmother will be "replacing" is living and consents (or is deceased), there should be no problem. If the biological parent is living and does not consent, the child cannot be adopted unless a court first terminates the biological parent's parental rights—usually on a finding that the biological parent is unfit.

The definition of unfitness varies from state to state. Normally it includes not only parents who have been abusive, neglectful, or convicted of serious crimes, but also parents who failed to support their children and have regular contact with them. In addition, severe, chronic mental illness also can make a parent unfit.

If a stepparent who adopted a child and the biological parent later obtain a divorce, the divorce does not affect the adoption. The step-parent continues to have all the rights and responsibilities of a biological parent, including a right to seek custody or visitation and a duty to support the child.

Similarly, an adopted child has all the rights of a biological child, including the right to inherit. If the child's adoptive parent leaves a will providing for his or her "children" without naming the individual children, the adopted child would be treated the same as a biological child. If an adoptive parent died without leaving a will, the adoptive child would receive the same share of inheritance under state law as a biological child would receive.

Depending on the complexity of local court procedures and the willingness of court personnel to explain what needs to be done, persons seeking to arrange a related adoption may be able to handle the procedure themselves without an attorney. Adoption procedures usually involve filing a written petition requesting the adoption, notifying persons who would be affected by the adoption (including the biological parents if they are alive), and appearing in court for a hearing. If the child is above a certain age (such as twelve), the child's consent also may be necessary.

UNRELATED ADOPTIONS

Unrelated adoptions (in which the person adopting the child is not related to the child or to the child's other parent) usually require more paperwork and more time to complete. Unrelated adoptions generally are of one of two types: an **agency adoption** or a **private adoption.**

AGENCY ADOPTIONS

In agency adoptions, as the name implies, the parents work through a licensed agency. The agency often supervises the care of biological mothers who are willing to give up their children, and it assists in the placement of children after birth. Agencies screen adoptive parents—

often extensively—before the adoption proceeds. Some agencies have long waiting lists of parents. Some agencies also specialize in placing children born in foreign countries.

Agencies generally are licensed and regulated by the state. An agency is more likely than persons handling private adoptions to offer counseling or support services to the adoptive family or the biological parents after completion of the adoption.

Adoption agencies are listed in the Yellow Pages, often under "Adoption."

PRIVATE ADOPTIONS

Private adoptions bypass agencies, and they may help bypass the long waiting lists as well. Private adoptions are available in most states, but not all.

The process of private adoptions may begin when people who seek to adopt a child contact an attorney who specializes in adoptions. The attorney may work with physicians who are aware of women willing to give up children for adoption. Sometimes would-be parents will place ads in newspapers, seeking women who are willing to place their babies for adoption. The ads might be placed by the adoptive parents directly or the ads might be placed by their attorney.

In most states, adoptive parents are allowed to pay a biological mother's medical expenses and certain other costs during the pregnancy. But adoptive parents are not allowed to pay the biological mother specifically to give up the child. The law treats this as a "black market adoption"—the buying and selling of children—and it's a crime in every state.

Court procedures vary from state to state, but in all states court approval is necessary for both agency and private adoptions. Many states also require that the adoptive parents be approved by a social service agency.

It is very important that proper consent be obtained from the biological parents. (That issue is discussed in the next two sections.) Assistance from an attorney in the state in which the adoption will take place is advisable.

Biological mother's consent. The biological mother must consent to the adoption, or her parental rights must have been terminated for other reasons such as abuse or neglect of the child. It is common for biological mothers who are planning to give up their children to sign a consent form before the child is born. The initial consent form, however, is not binding.

The mother has the right to revoke her consent for a certain period of time after the child is born. In most states, that time period is relatively short, such as forty-eight to seventy-two hours, although some states may allow a longer period in which a mother may revoke her consent. (Legislation called the **Uniform Adoption Act**, which may be enacted in some states, allows a biological mother eight days from birth of the child to revoke her consent.)

BE SURE THE FATHER CONSENTS

Failure to obtain consent from the biological father has been at the center of some highly publicized adoption cases. In the Illinois case of **Baby Richard**, for example, the biological mother conceived a child out of wedlock. At the time of Baby Richard's birth, the biological mother and biological father were not living together. The mother lied to the father and told him that their child had died.

Meanwhile, the mother consented to termination of her parental rights and to adoption of the child. Later, the biological father learned the child was alive, and he sought to undo the adoption and gain custody of Baby Richard. The father filed his claim for custody fifty-seven days after Baby Richard's birth.

The case dragged through the Illinois courts for years while the child lived with his adoptive parents. When "Baby" Richard was three years old, the Illinois Supreme Court ruled that Richard must be returned to his biological father, since the father never consented to the adoption and contested the adoption within two months of Richard's birth. The Illinois Supreme Court refused to consider the quality of the child's relationship with the adoptive

---

If a biological mother consented to adoption during the proper period of time after birth, it is much harder for her to revoke her consent. Following an after-birth consent, a biological mother generally may revoke her consent only if she can show that there was **fraud** or **duress**. Fraud could be found if the adoption agency or attorney lied to the biological mother about the consequences of what she was doing. Duress might exist if a person at the adoption agency threatened the biological mother with humiliation if she did not sign.

A biological mother's change of heart normally is not enough by itself to revoke an after-birth adoption consent. Although a mother may feel emotionally drained and under stress after birth of a child that she plans to give up for adoption, that type of stress usually is not enough to revoke an adoption unless the person or agency that obtained the mother's consent used harsh tactics to obtain her consent.

parents or what was best for Richard. Instead, the court held the biological father was entitled to custody.

The court's decision caused an uproar in Illinois. The governor and many legislators objected to the decision. Although feeling some sympathy for the biological father who was deceived about the birth of his son, many people felt the rights of the child and adoptive parents should be paramount. The legislature passed a statute requiring courts to consider the best interest of a child when deciding whether to rescind an adoption. The Illinois Supreme Court refused to apply the statute to Richard's case and still ordered that Richard be returned to the biological father.

The case of Baby Richard illustrates the importance of obtaining consent of the biological father in order to help ensure the adoption will not be undone. If a father who is not notified of his child's existence contests the adoption within the time period designated by state law, the adoptive parents might lose custody of the child. Many states are considering laws that would give greater protection to the adoptive parents and to adoptive children who have bonded with their adoptive parents. But in the meantime, many states place more emphasis on the rights of the biological father than the interests of the child or the adoptive parents.

Biological father's consent. A biological father's consent also is necessary for adoption—at least if the father is known. The biological father should be notified of the birth and pending adoption so that he may consent or object. If the father is not known, the adoption may proceed without his consent (although adoptive parents can feel safer about the validity of their adoption if the biological father has been notified and agreed to it).

If a biological father is not notified, he may later contest the adoption if he acts within a certain period of time after the child's birth or adoption. (Six months is a typical time period, although the period varies between states.)

OTHER ADOPTION ISSUES

FOREIGN ADOPTIONS

With the shortage of healthy, white infants and the lengthy wait for adoptions through many American adoption agencies, some prospective parents look to other countries for an adoptable child. If a couple (or an individual) is seeking a child through this route, it is best to work with an agency or an attorney experienced in foreign adoptions with particular experience in the country from which the child is being sought. The adoptive parents will have to deal not only with U.S. regulations, but also regulations of the country from which the child comes.

Depending on how the adoption is set up, the child might be adopted by the American couple in the country where the child was born and then brought to the United States, or the child might be brought to the United States with adoption proceedings taking place in an American court. Either way, entry of the child into the United States will need to be cleared by the U.S. Immigration and Naturalization Service (INS).

The INS requires that the adoptive parents have a home study by a licensed social worker and that the child receive a medical exam before being brought into the United States.

The INS also requires proof that the child is an **orphan**, which means that the biological parents are dead or that they voluntarily gave up the child. If such documentation cannot be obtained, the adoptive parents may find themselves stranded with the child in the child's home country until documentation is obtained or a waiver is issued. In some countries, the persons or agencies providing children for adoption may submit forged documents in connection with an adoption. If the INS suspects forgery, this may delay the process further.

INTERRACIAL ADOPTIONS

Among the controversial issues in adoption law is interracial adoptions—particularly adoption of African-American children by white parents. In 1972 a spokesperson for the Association of Black Social Workers condemned interracial adoptions as "racial genocide." The organization has continued to oppose interracial adoptions.

Proponents of interracial adoptions note that there are tens of thousand of black children in foster care available for adoption, but there are not enough black families available to adopt them. Proponents of interracial adoption argue that a child is better off being adopted by a family of a different race than not being adopted at all.

The trend in the law is to allow race to be a factor in adoptions, but not to allow race to completely block or indefinitely delay adoptions of children who are members of minority groups. If, for example, a black family is available to adopt a black child, the black family generally will be preferred over a white family. But if a black family were not available to adopt the child, the child should be eligible for placement with a white family.

A bill under consideration by Congress would prohibit adoption agencies that receive federal funds from delaying adoption or placement of children in foster care on the basis of race or nationality.

OPEN ADOPTION

An **open adoption** is one in which the adoptive parents agree to let the biological mother (or biological father) have continued contact with the child after the adoption. This contact may consist of periodic visits or an exchange of pictures and other information between the adoptive family and the biological parent or parents. The nature of the contact often is specified in the adoption agreement. Open adoptions have become more common as more birth mothers are involved with choosing which adoptive family will receive their children (particularly through private adoptions).

Open adoptions are a relatively new phenomenon, and in many states the laws are not clear regarding whether an open adoption agreement is enforceable by the birth mother (or father) in the event the adoptive parents seek to discontinue contact with the biological parents.

ADOPTION BY SINGLE PEOPLE OR SAME-SEX COUPLES

Single-parent adoptions. Single persons may adopt children, although some agencies strongly prefer to place a child with a married couple. Other agencies—particularly those dealing with children who might be hard to place—are willing to place a child with a single person. Single-parent adoptions usually are possible in private adoptions.

As with adoptions sought by a couple, a single person who seeks to adopt a child must be approved by a social service investigator and show that appropriate arrangements have been made for care of the child.

Adoption by lesbian or gay couples. Some states—including New York and California—allow gay and lesbian couples to adopt a child. Other states do not allow such adoptions, and many states have laws that are unclear regarding whether it is permissible for two persons of the same sex to adopt a child.

The uncertainty comes from the nature of traditional adoption laws. Adoption laws generally require that the parental rights of the biological parents be terminated. Termination of parental rights traditionally has meant that the biological parents have no more rights or responsibilities regarding the child. If the birth parent is seeking to maintain contact with the child, that might be viewed as an impermissible assertion of rights that no longer exist.

On the other hand, if the adoptive parents had agreed to contact with the biological parent and the adoption was contingent on such contact, the agreement might be enforceable. A biological parent should not count on such agreements being enforceable unless state law clearly says so.

ADOPTION RECORDS

In most states, a court's adoption records are sealed and can be opened only by court order. Procedures and standards for opening records vary by state. Increasingly, states require that certain non-identifying information, such as the medical history of the biological family, be made available to the adoptive parents at the time of adoption.

Some states have registries where parties to the adoption can seek to contact each other. If, for example, a biological mother seeks to find out about her child she may place her name, address, and telephone number with the registry. If the adopted child (or adoptive parent) seeks contact with the biological parents, they may place their names in the registry. If a registry official determines there is a "match" of people seeking information about each other, the registry will provide information to facilitate the contact.

LEGAL ACTION FOR "WRONGFUL ADOPTION"

Under the law of many states, if an adoption agency has adverse information about a child who is being considered for adoption, the agency has an obligation to pass on the information to the prospective adoptive family, particularly if the prospective adoptive family asks for such information. Adverse information could include a serious illness of the child that is not readily apparent to the adoptive parents. If the agency does not provide the information, the agency could be liable for the damages that result. A lawsuit for such damages sometimes is referred to as an action for **wrongful adoption**.

In one case, for example, an agency withheld information about the biological mother's mental illness and institutionalization. As the child grew, the parents realized the child had a severe mental illness requiring substantial treatment. The adoptive parents were able to collect damages for the cost of treatment and for their own emotional suffering.

In states that allow adoptive parents to seek damages from agencies for a "wrongful adoption," the law does not require that the agency guarantee the quality of a child—like a car dealer would guarantee a new car—but the law does require that if the agency knows significant adverse information about the child, the agency must share that information with the adoptive parents.

■

CHAPTER SEVEN

Deciding Whether or Not to Divorce

T HE LEAD FEATURE in each issue of *Ladies' Home Journal* is a column entitled "Can This Marriage Be Saved?"[1] which the *Journal* bills as "the most popular, enduring women's magazine feature in the world."

The feature has three sections. The first section is "The Wife's Turn" in which the wife recounts the frustrations of her marriage and why she is considering leaving it. Second, the husband takes his turn and talks about his unhappiness. (The husband usually comes across as being more at fault than the wife.) Third, the counselor takes a turn and analyzes how the couple reached an impasse and what can be done to save the marriage. In *Ladies' Home Journal,* the marriage always is saved.

In real life, marriage counselors, of course, do not save all marriages, but they can help save some marriages, and they also can help wives and husbands with individual growth regardless of whether they decide to divorce.

The decision to divorce usually is not an easy one. It is common to go through periods of ambivalence when deciding whether or not to stay with a marriage. The ultimate decision may be based on a combination of logic, intuition, and gut feeling.

---

[1] "Can This Marriage Be Saved" is a registered trademark of Meredith Corporation. The ideas presented in this section are drawn from a variety of books and journals. Among them are *Bailing Out* by Barry Lubetkin, Ph.D. and Elena Oumano, Ph.D. (Fireside Books, 1993) and *Learning to Leave—A Woman's Guide* by Lynette Triere with Richard Peacock (Warner-Books, 1993).

Placing structure on the decision-making process can be helpful. If you are considering divorce, you might benefit from making a series of lists. The first two lists could be reasons to stay married and reasons to divorce. The reasons would include what you like and don't like about your spouse as well as other factors, such as impact on your children, impact on your relationships with extended family and friends, financial security, and day-to-day needs and services provided by your spouse.

You'll note that not all items on the lists are of equal weight. You might try a quantitative approach—assigning a number value to each item on the lists ("5" for high importance; "3" for middle importance; and "1" for low importance). Add the columns. See how the numbers compare. Put the lists away for a while, and then look at them again to see if there are other factors or changes in the importance of items on the lists.

Another list (somewhat related to the first two) is a set of goals for your life. Try to list all the important goals—perhaps a warm, sharing relationship with a mate; happy, productive children; time with friends; a satisfying job; travel; recreational activities. Then go through the list again and try to figure out how staying with your mate will advance or interfere with the goals, and, conversely, how a divorce will advance or interfere with those goals.

When a marriage is in a rocky period, it is common after yet another fight or another humiliation to think, "I can't take this anymore! I've got to get out of this relationship!" The time may come when that is true, but the negative times also may be part of a cycle that needs to be placed in perspective.

One way of gaining that perspective is to keep a log or make marks on a calendar regarding how you feel—about your spouse, your marriage, yourself, or life in general. Make brief notations (perhaps in code if you are worried about discovery) about how you feel each day. Keep the log for a month or two and then look at the overall picture. Do the bad days really outnumber the good? Is there a pattern to the good days or bad? Do the same issues arise?

One cautionary note about keeping logs or diaries: In some states these might be subject to **discovery** in court litigation—meaning that your spouse and your spouse's attorney may be able to order you to produce the logs and diaries for their inspection because the documents might be relevant to some issue in the case. In other states, logs and diaries could be protected under a right of privacy or under rules that keep confidential any documents that you prepare to help your attorney with the case.

The decision of whether or not to divorce boils down to the question: "Am I better off with my spouse or without my spouse?" The answer lies not only in how you feel about your a spouse and how your spouse feels about you, but also in an assessment of how your total life will be different after a divorce. There may be prospects for a better romantic relationship after a divorce, but other things will be different too. Will that total cluster of differences be a net improvement or a net deficit?

On the subject of hope for a better woman-man relationship in the future, take inventory of the reasons for the breakdown of the current relationship and try to assess if you truly have the perspectives and skills for a better relationship next time around.

A clear perspective on what went wrong is hard to achieve. It takes some genuine soul-searching with careful attention to patterns that developed in relationships with parents early in life. Many therapists have noted that people seem to have an unconscious radar that draws them to mates who have significant characteristics in common with their parents—particularly the negative characteristics.

Husbands and wives who had conflictual relationships with parents may have vowed not to marry someone with a particular problem. The husband and wife may (or may not) have avoided that problem, but often they zeroed in on a mate who duplicates some other problems from their earlier home environments. There is comfort—perhaps unconscious comfort—in things that are familiar, even if the result is conflict.

Before heading out on a new path in the quest to feel whole, it is best to be sure the path will be a better one.

There is no precise, foolproof formula for deciding whether or not to divorce. Many counselors, however, agree that there are certain circumstances in which divorce is often the best solution. A divorce may be the best solution if you are married to a person who is abusive; addicted to alcohol, drugs, or gambling; or severely mentally ill.

Even in these circumstances, there is the added question: "Is your spouse genuinely willing to seek professional help?" If so, there may be a relationship worth saving. The spouse, however, must actually seek help and stick with it. A mere promise to change followed by a few days of improved conduct is not enough.

Describing more subjective factors in the decision to divorce, psychiatrist Dr. Peter Martin has written in *The Ann Landers Encyclopedia A to Z,* "In my experience there are only a few factors that would make a marriage impossible to save. One is the absence in both mates of the ability to feel sympathy for the other. This is usually accompanied by a deep unchanging hatred."

Monitoring your own well-being is another indicator of the need for divorce or making other changes. If you chronically feel sad or if you have low energy, trouble sleeping, and a difficult time focusing on day-to-day tasks, that probably is depression. Similarly, if you are developing anxieties or phobias about things that did not bother you before, or if you are physically ill more frequently than before, these too are signs of trouble. Professional help from a physician or therapist can help, along with an evaluation of how much of the problem is related to the marriage.

For many people contemplating divorce, there is not a single, dramatic circumstance that leads to consideration of divorce. For them, the problems do not include abuse, addiction, or mental illness. Instead, there is a growing malaise (coupled with anger)—a growing sense that the marriage is not working and that the relationship is draining more energy than it is giving back.

For many couples, the primary problem is communication.

This book is not a detailed "how-to" manual on healing an injured marriage. There are dozens of books on that subject. But it is worth recapping some of the main themes of marriage counselors on how to improve a marriage. Unless the need to get out of the marriage is urgent, these steps can be useful:

- Try talking again with your spouse about your feelings. Focus on your feelings and on your partner's feelings. Talk about what makes you happy or sad—what you each need. Start with subjects that are relatively noncontroversial and work up to more sensitive topics.

- Recognize that if you or your spouse came from a family where feelings were suppressed or punished, it is hard to talk freely about how one feels. But also recognize that neither one of you is a mind reader. If you want your spouse to understand how you feel and what you'd like, you have to communicate.

- Talk in a way that is nonaccusatory. Name-calling and listing the other's faults just adds to the anger and usually misses the heart of the issues. Humiliating or demeaning each other is not going to solve the problem.

- If anger erupts, take "time out." Leave the room for a while; take a deep breath; count to ten; hold off discussion of the issue until the next day. Don't respond in anger, but do tell your partner what makes you angry.

- In addition to avoiding verbal anger, watch body language. A sneer or rolling of eyes can have the same counterproductive effect as a verbal assault.

- To help make sure you each understand what the other is saying, structure the conversations so that you each listen carefully. Allow each of you to speak uninterrupted for a few minutes. After one of you has spoken, have the other repeat the essence of what was said—without commenting on what was said. The goal at this point is to ensure that you each understand what the other has said and felt, not to reach agreement on a particular issue.

- Talk about why you feel a certain way. Recall your relationships with parents, siblings, or former spouses. Think about why you may have an emotional allergy to certain things your spouse has done or said. Your "allergic" reaction may be more severe than "normal" but nonetheless quite understandable when you (and your spouse) see where the reaction is coming from.

- If you have fallen into the habit of not spending private time together and really talking, schedule some time. Take a walk; go on a weekend vacation; schedule a series of half hours in the evening (but not so late in the evening that you are too tired). If you have children, hire a sitter and go out by yourselves. If you can't afford a sitter, perhaps a friend or family member can watch the children for a while.

- Find out what little things would make the other happy. Do them (and try to come up with a few things of your own initiative.) Work up to bigger things.

Marriage counseling can be useful. Counselors can be found through a variety of sources, including: family physicians, hospital referral services, crisis intervention programs, religious institutions, other community service programs, friends, and the Yellow Pages (usually under "Marriage Counselors").

Marriage counseling does not guarantee saving a marriage. In order for a marriage to work well, it takes commitment by both partners as well as a reasonably good match in the first place.

Even if marriage counseling does not save the marriage, a good counselor can facilitate communication and clarify issues. If the marriage is going to end, marriage counseling can be converted into "divorce counseling"—helping the parties to get out of the marriage while minimizing harm to themselves and their children.

IMPACT OF DIVORCE ON SPOUSES

Divorce, of course, is a stressful time in a person's life. Emotional reactions include depression, anger, jealousy, humiliation, disorientation, and sense of loss.

The sense of loss arises not only from loss of positive aspects of a marriage, but also from loss of negative aspects of a marriage. Divorce researchers Andre Derdeyn and Elizabeth Scott have written: "The sense of loss can be just as great if the relationship had long since been almost exclusively negative and conflictual . . . '[T]he intensity of grief is related to the intensity of involvement rather than of love.' For many spouses, the marriage—whether dominantly positive or negative—was an integral part of their emotional being, and the loss of the marriage can be very disruptive."

Judith Wallerstein and Joan Kelly, who research the effect of divorce on parents and children, found that the average time after a divorce for women to reestablish "inner equilibrium," "external stability," and "a sense of continuity in their lives" was three to three and a half years. For men, the average time to reestablish continuity was two to two and a half years. Men had a shorter recovery time than women because men, as a group, had more external supports, including greater financial security and job satisfaction, which help ease the transition process.

Although most spouses recover from divorce with the passage of time, some do not. For those who do not recover, the decline in adult functioning becomes chronic. Spouses who are not able to regain equilibrium often had their primary identity wrapped up in the marriage and have few inner or external resources on which to fall back.

In the time surrounding a divorce, as parents cope with their own wounds, it is common for parents to become more self-centered and less available to the child. In most (but not all) cases, parenting skills return to normal after a few years.

REACTION OF CHILDREN TO DIVORCE

One of a child's first reactions to divorce is fear of abandonment. The child reasons that if one parent can leave, then the other parent might leave too. The child needs steady reassurance that he or she will not be abandoned. Hopefully, the reassurance can come from both parents, ideally through substantial contact with both parents.

Young children also are concerned that the parent who is moving out will not be taken care of or will not have a place to stay. Some of those concerns can be alleviated by promptly showing the child where the departing dad or mom will live.

Other common reactions of children to divorce include sleep disturbances, fears of impending disaster, suspiciousness, under-achievement in school, poor peer relationships, emotional constriction, and regression in behavior (such as bed-wetting).

Many children feel powerless and vulnerable in the period during and following a divorce. Assuming the child liked both parents, the child wants to stop the divorce but cannot. Children often blame themselves for the divorce and think if they had done something different that their parents would not be divorcing.

Children need to be told—often many times—that the divorce is not their fault, that Dad and Mom are not living together because Dad and Mom could not get along, not because the child did something wrong.

Although nothing takes all the pain out of divorce for a child, Dr. Wallerstein notes that the manner in which children are told about a divorce will have a lasting effect on them. Certain ways of telling a child, such as saying, "He left *us*!" or "She does not love *us*!" will only maximize suffering.

Telling the child that the divorce will not make a difference in the child's life also is unwise. Obviously, the divorce will make a difference. The child should be given a simple, honest explanation of the divorce without lurid details designed to alienate the child from the other parent. The parents should explain what will be different and what will not be different—including talking about where the child will live, where the child will go to school, and when the child will be with each parent.

The child should be given an opportunity to express feelings and to ask questions. The child also might be told that things will be difficult for a while, but they will improve with the passage of time.

Studies have shown that one of the most important factors for a child's recovery is a close, ongoing relationship with both parents.

DECIDING TO PROCEED WITH A DIVORCE

As discussed in the opening section of this chapter, the process of deciding whether to divorce can be filled with ambivalence and anxiety. When the decision to divorce is reached, however, it also can be a time of relief.

In their book *Bailing Out*, authors Barry Lubetkin and Elena Oumano comment, " '[B]ailing out' when you know your relationship is no longer viable can be one of the most affirmative, liberating acts of one's life. Bailing out can be a wonderful growth experience *if* you use this period of your life as a time to explore, discover, and evaluate beliefs that have determined your behavior . . . The irrefutable fact is that staying with someone in a miserable or indifferent relationship, whether in a marriage or a live-in situation, erodes your self-esteem."

Ann Landers echoed part of that view in *The Ann Landers Encyclopedia A to Z*: "Life is too precious to waste years in a joyless marriage—or, worse yet, in a miserable one."

When you have decided to divorce (or have a strong inclination to divorce), a question of timing may remain: When do you announce the decision or take additional steps such as separating or filing a legal action? The answer lies in balancing the stresses of maintaining the *status quo* versus the benefits of waiting.

Sometimes it is best to wait. If you are feeling emotionally spent and do not have plans on how to proceed, it may be useful to pause while building emotional energy and planning the next phase of your life. Steps to take include:

1. deciding where you want to live
2. figuring out options on custody if you have children
3. determining if changes related to employment are likely to be necessary
4. planning a budget (or range of budgets, depending on how the divorce proceeds)
5. lining up a lawyer if one is necessary
6. cementing ties with friends, family, and other support networks during your time of transition

The many issues on which to work may seem daunting, but when they are taken one step at a time, they are manageable.

Talking with friends who have gone through a divorce can be helpful. In addition to providing emotional support, friends also can offer perspectives on how to cope with the changes.

Advance planning has psychological advantages. A study of a group of women found that the length of time between the decision to divorce and marital separation was positively associated with the ability to adjust to divorce. In other words, the longer the period between the decision to divorce and the separation, the better the adjustment (although it is possible to have a good adjustment in a short period of time too).

Embarking on a new path is a time for renewal. Most people in an unhappy marriage at some point stopped being involved in certain activities that once brought them pleasure, or they did not pursue other activities that they always wanted to do. Now is the chance.

The new outlets may be a recreational activity, a college course, theater, more time with friends, or just quiet evenings at home by yourself.

Divorce is a beginning as well as an end.

■

CHAPTER EIGHT

Separation, Annulment, and Divorce

APPROXIMATELY HALF OF ALL MARRIAGES in the United States end in divorce. The current divorce rate is down a few percentage points from a peak in the early 1980s, but the current divorce rate is almost double what it was in the 1950s. (See graph on page 63.)

As discussed in chapter 3, the state sets the requirements for creating a marriage. The state also sets the requirements for ending a marriage, but the regulations are more complicated, since there are more issues to sort out when a marriage ends than when it begins. (Perhaps if before marriage, prospective husbands and wives spent more time exploring issues they will have to deal with during marriage, the divorce rate would be lower.)

SEPARATION AND SEPARATE MAINTENANCE

Separation, as the term implies, means the wife and husband are living apart. The wife and husband generally are not required to separate in order to obtain a divorce, although for psychological reasons, it usually works out that way. In some states, certain grounds for divorce may require that the parties live apart for a specified period of time, but in most states there are grounds for divorce that do not require a period of separation.

A **legal separation** also means the husband and wife are living apart, but a legal separation has the added element that the arrangement is ordered by the court or consented to by the parties in a written agreement. The fact that the separation is part of a court order or written agreement makes it a "*legal* separation."

The main reason for obtaining a legal separation instead of an informal separation is to make more certain the rights and responsibilities of the parties during the period of separation. If one party—usually the wife—will be receiving financial support during the period of separation, the court order or written agreement will make such support an enforceable right.

Payments of support during a period of separation sometimes are called **separate maintenance** or **alimony pendente lite**. If the person obliged to make such payments fails to do so, a court could order the payments and take steps to enforce payments.

Written agreements regarding support are necessary if the person making the payments wishes to claim a tax deduction for paying

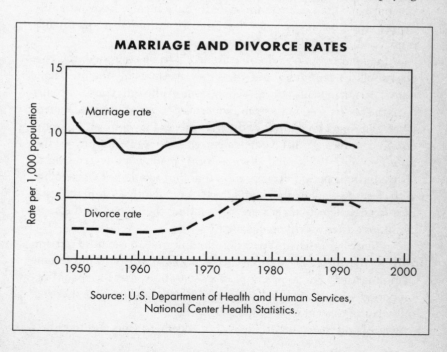

MARRIAGE AND DIVORCE RATES

Rate per 1,000 population

Marriage rate

Divorce rate

Source: U.S. Department of Health and Human Services,
National Center Health Statistics.

support to the spouse. If the person paying support obtains a deduction for the amount paid, then the same amount will be treated as taxable income to the recipient. Without a written agreement or court order, the payments of support will not be deductible to the payer, nor would they be treated as income to the recipient. (For more discussion of the tax aspects of one spouse making support payments to the other, see chapter 10 on "Alimony/Maintenance.")

If the husband and wife have children, the separation agreement or court order can specify arrangements regarding custody or visitation with the children, and those arrangements also can be enforced by the court.

A separation (or legal separation) is not the same as a divorce. Persons who are separated may not remarry. They must wait until a divorce is final before being able to remarry. The terms of a separation agreement usually can be modified by the court or by the parties themselves during the period of separation.

Courts, or the husband and wife by agreement, also can modify the provisions of support, custody, and visitation when the divorce is finalized.

If the final terms of a divorce are likely to be contested, the parties should be cautious about what they accept as a voluntary, temporary arrangement during separation. Although courts usually have the power to depart from the terms of a separation agreement when entering a final order of divorce, judges may look at the *status quo* and think, "If this arrangement was workable during separation, it should work after divorce too." If someone is agreeing to terms during a period of separation that they would not want to live with after the divorce, they should make abundantly clear in the separation agreement that they are not binding themselves to the same conditions after the divorce is final.

An informal or legal separation does not mean the husband and wife must divorce. They are free to reconcile at any time and resume living together. For some couples, a separation serves as a cooling-off period—a method of relieving immediate pressure while they sort out what they want to do with their lives.

If husband and wife decide to live together again and there is a court action pending, the action should be **dismissed** (at least after the couple is reasonably sure they will stay together). "Dismissed" means the case is taken off the list of active cases before the court. If the couple does not dismiss their pending case, the court usually will dismiss the case automatically if nothing has been done on the case after a certain period of time (such as six months to one year). If the husband or wife later decides to divorce, the case can be refiled.

ANNULMENT

An **annulment** is a court ruling that a supposed marriage was never valid. The most common ground for annulment is fraud. For example, one person may have not disclosed to the other a prior divorce, a criminal record, or an unwillingness to have sexual intercourse. An annulment also may be granted if one of the parties to the "marriage" was still married to someone else at the time of the marriage that is at issue. Other bases for annulments include marriage of an underage person, marriage to too close a blood relative, and marriage by a person under duress at the time of marriage.

Annulments are uncommon compared to divorces because divorces are easy to obtain and the bases for an annulment are much narrower than the bases for a divorce. One party may prefer an annulment, however, in order to avoid some of the financial obligations that a court might impose in a divorce. For more discussion of legal annulments, see chapter 3.

Aside from annulments granted by a court, some parties to a marriage also may seek a religious annulment of a marriage. A few religions will not permit a member of the faith to enter into a marriage if the member already had one valid marriage. In that circumstance, a person who was divorced would not be permitted to remarry, since the divorce implies that a valid marriage existed. However, if the member was able to obtain a declaration by religious court or religious official that the first marriage was not valid, then the member may be free to marry.

If a person seeking a divorce (or legal annulment) is concerned about the ability to remarry within his or her faith, that person should seek an agreement or court order that the former spouse will cooperate in obtaining a religious annulment or religious divorce.

DIVORCE

A **divorce**—referred to in some states as a **dissolution of marriage**—is a decree by a court that a valid marriage no longer exists. A divorce leaves both parties free to remarry. It usually provides for division of property and makes arrangements for child custody and support.

Although divorces may be emotionally contentious, most divorces (probably more than 95 percent) do not end up in a contested trial. Usually the parties negotiate and settle such things as division of property, spousal support, and child custody between themselves, often with an attorney's help. Sometimes parties reach an agreement by mediation, with a trained mediator who tries to help husband and wife identify and accommodate common interests. The parties then present their negotiated or mediated agreement to a judge. Approval is virtually automatic if the agreement appears to meet a minimal standard of fairness.

If parties are unable to agree about property, support, and child custody, they may ask the court to decide one or more of those issues. Chapters 9 through 12 will discuss how courts decide those issues.

A threshold requirement for obtaining a divorce in most states is **residency** or **domicile** of one or both parties who are to be divorced. "Residency" refers to the state in which a person lives; "domicile" refers to the state that the person regards as "home." Usually the state of a person's residency and domicile are the same, but sometimes they can be different. For example, a couple may reside four months each year in the state of their "summer home," but regard another state where they spend the rest of the year as their true home (and that state would be the state of their domicile).

Residency (or domicile) requirements vary. A few states have no residency requirement. In those states, a person can arrive and seek a divorce on the same day. Residency requirements of other states range from six weeks to one year; six months is the most common time period. In those states, a party must have lived in the state for the specified period before a divorce can be granted.

The party seeking a divorce must state a ground for divorce in the papers filed with the court. The grounds may be based on **no-fault** or **fault**, depending on the state. All states now offer no-fault divorces; approximately thirty-one states also offer fault-based grounds as an additional option. (See chart on pages 68 to 69.)

A no-fault divorce is a divorce in which neither the wife nor husband officially blames the other for breakdown of the marriage. There are no accusations necessary to obtain a divorce—no need to prove "guilt" or "fault." Common bases for a no-fault divorce are "irreconcilable differences," "irretrievable breakdown," or "incompatibility." As those terms imply, the marriage is considered to be over, but the court and the legal documents do not try to assign blame.

Another common basis for a no-fault divorce is that the parties have lived separately for a certain period of time, such as for six months or a year, with the intent that the separation be permanent.

Over the last thirty years, "no-fault" has replaced "fault" as the dominant basis for obtaining a divorce. No-fault divorces are considered a more humane and realistic way to end a marriage. Husbands and wives who are divorcing usually are suffering enough without adding more fuel to the emotional fires by trying to prove who did what to whom. The laws of no-fault divorce recognize that human relationships are complex and that it is difficult to prove that a marriage broke down solely because of what one person did.

Some critics of no-fault divorces are concerned that an economically dependent spouse may not be adequately protected when it is so easy for the other spouse to obtain a divorce. The critics argue that no-fault divorces result in lower awards of property and support to economically dependent spouses than fault-based divorces. Proof of cause-and-effect on this issue is far from certain.

In the states that allow divorces based on fault (in addition to no-fault divorces), the grounds for fault-based divorces vary. Here is the laundry list (one might say dirty laundry list) of grounds:

1. adultery
2. physical cruelty
3. mental cruelty
4. attempted murder

GROUNDS FOR DIVORCE

	No-Fault Sole Ground	No-Fault Added to Traditional Factors	Residency/ Domicile Requirements
Alabama		x	6 months
Alaska		x	None
Arizona	x		90 days
Arkansas		x	60 days
California	x		6 months
Colorado	x		90 days
Connecticut		x	1 year
Delaware	x		6 months
D.C.	x		6 months
Florida	x		6 months
Georgia		x	6 months
Hawaii	x		6 months
Idaho		x	6 weeks
Illinois		x	90 days
Indiana		x	6 months
Iowa	x		None
Kansas			60 days
Kentucky	x		180 days
Louisiana		x	None
Maine		x	6 months
Maryland		x	1 year
Massachusetts		x	None
Michigan	x		6 months
Minnesota	x		180 days
Mississippi		x	6 months

5. desertion
6. habitual drunkenness
7. use of addictive drugs
8. insanity

9. impotency (usually unknown to the partner at the time of marriage)
10. infection of one's spouse with venereal disease

	No-Fault Sole Ground	No-Fault Added to Traditional Factors	Residency/ Domicile Requirements
Missouri	x		90 days
Montana	x		90 days
Nebraska	x		1 year
Nevada			6 weeks
New Hampshire		x	1 year
New Jersey		x	1 year
New Mexico		x	6 months
New York		x	1 year
North Carolina		x	6 months
North Dakota		x	6 months
Ohio		x	6 months
Oklahoma		x	6 months
Oregon	x		6 months
Pennsylvania		x	6 months
Rhode Island		x	1 year
South Carolina		x	3 months
South Dakota		x	None
Tennessee		x	6 months
Texas		x	6 months
Utah		x	90 days
Vermont		x	6 months
Virginia		x	6 months
Washington	x		1 year
West Virginia		x	1 year
Wisconsin	x		6 months
Wyoming	x		60 days

Source: *ABA Family Law Quarterly.*

Husbands or wives in the mood for revenge probably could come up with a multicount complaint. Some spouses want the emotional release of proving fault by their mates. But courts are not a very good forum for such personal issues, and the accuser is usually less satisfied than he or she expected to be. The degree to which "fault" affects division of property, support, and custody will be discussed in the chapters on those subjects.

RESUMPTION OF UNMARRIED NAME

A woman who divorces may resume her unmarried name or keep her married name as she wishes. She can even change her name to something completely new, as long as she is not doing so for fraudulent purposes. Court proceedings generally are not necessary in order to change a name.

If a woman is changing her name, she should notify government agencies and private companies that have records of her name. Examples of places to notify: the Internal Revenue Service, Social Security Administration, Passport Agency (within U.S. State Department), Post Office, state tax agencies, driver's license bureau, voter registration bureau, professional licensing agencies, professional societies, unions, mortgage companies, landlord, banks, charge card companies, telephone companies, other utilities, magazines and newspapers to which she subscribes, doctors and dentists, and schools and colleges that she attended or that her children attend.

It can be useful to have the divorce decree state that the wife will resume her unmarried name, but generally it is not necessary to do so in order for a woman to make a valid name change.

■

CHAPTER NINE

Dividing Property

IN THE EVENT OF DIVORCE, the husband and wife generally are free to divide their property as they see fit. They may enter into what is called a **marital settlement agreement**. A marital settlement agreement is a contract between the husband and wife that divides property and debts and resolves other issues of the divorce. Although many divorces begin with a high level of acrimony, a substantial majority of divorces (95 percent or more) are settled by the husband and wife—often with help from attorneys—without need for a judge deciding property issues or other issues.

When the husband and wife have reached a marital settlement agreement, they can take the agreement to court, where a judge usually will approve the agreement after a short hearing. Some states with simplified divorce procedures might not even require a hearing if everything has been agreed to by the husband and wife.

Settlement agreements operate in what is sometimes called **the shadow of the law**—meaning that parties and their attorneys are aware of what a judge might do if a judge had to decide the case. It may not be possible to predict with complete precision what a judge would do, but an experienced attorney can give a range of possible results. With that knowledge, parties often prefer to reach their own agreements rather than go through the monetary and emotional expense of a trial.

DECIDING WHETHER TO GO TO TRIAL

The decision of whether or not to go to trial and to have a judge decide contested issues often involves a cost-benefit analysis. If the financial benefit that may be received from going to trial is high compared to the cost of going to trial, it may make sense to go to trial. For example, if wife and husband dispute the value of a business started by the husband during the marriage and the difference in their valuations is substantial, then it may make sense to let a judge decide the issue rather than give in to an unreasonable valuation by the other side.

The parties will need to look at the facts objectively. How much attorney time will it take to develop facts about the business? How much will it cost to hire an expert to evaluate the business and testify at trial? If, after gathering preliminary information and trying negotiations, the husband still says the business is worth $50,000 and the wife still believes the business is worth $1 million, the only way to solve the problem may be to go to court. (Chapter 15 discusses meditation and other alternative means of resolving disputes.)

On the other hand, if the business is a very small one, with the husband saying it is worth $10,000 and the wife saying it is worth $15,000, it does not make sense for one or both sides to spend $10,000 in attorneys' fees and experts' fees to try to ascertain a precise value of the business.

SEPARATE OR NONMARITAL PROPERTY

The laws of dividing property vary from state to state. As a starting point, however, most states allow parties to keep their own **separate or nonmarital property.** Nonmarital property includes property that a spouse brought into the marriage and kept separate during the marriage. It also includes inheritances received during the marriage and kept separate during the marriage. In addition, nonmarital or separate property may include gifts received by just one spouse during the marriage. A few states permit division of separate as well as marital property when parties divorce, but the origin of the property is considered when deciding who receives the property.

The right of a spouse to keep his or her separate or nonmarital property may depend on the degree to which the property was, in fact, kept separate. For example, if a wife came into a marriage with a $20,000 money market account and wanted to keep it as nonmarital property, she should keep the account in her own name and not deposit any funds earned during the marriage into the account. She should not, for instance, deposit her paychecks directly into the money market account, because the paychecks are marital funds and could turn the whole account into marital property. (Marital property will be explained in the next section.) The process of changing nonmarital property into marital property and vice versa sometimes is called **transmutation** (from Latin words meaning "cross" and "change").

Another example: If a husband inherits some stock from his mother during the marriage and he wants to keep it as nonmarital property, he should open his own investment account and should not use the account for any investments that he and his wife own together. If a husband or wife decides to use some nonmarital funds for a common purpose, such as purchasing a home in joint tenancy, that money normally will become marital property. The nonmarital property will be viewed by the courts of most states as a gift to the marriage.

Similarly, if a wife or husband takes nonmarital funds and places them in a joint checking account, the funds generally will become

---

ENGAGEMENT RINGS

If an engagement is broken off, what happens to the engagement ring? Normally it should be returned to the person who gave it. The ring usually is viewed as a gift given in anticipation of marriage. If the marriage will not take place, the condition upon which the gift was given has been removed, so the gift should be returned.

If the parties have given each other presents during their relationship—such as birthday presents or holiday presents—those gifts normally do not have to be returned. Those presents usually would be viewed as unconditional gifts, such as those between friends. Once the gift is given, the recipient is entitled to keep it, unless the person making the gift placed a clear condition when presenting the gift.

marital property. In some states, the presumption that funds placed in a joint account are marital property can be overcome by specific proof that the spouse depositing the funds did not intend to have the funds used for a marital purpose. Nonetheless, if a husband or wife does not want nonmarital property converted into marital property, it is best to keep the nonmarital property separate. Always.

Property distribution laws have many intricacies and variations between states; understanding them usually requires a lawyer's help. For example, in many states, the increase in value of nonmarital property (such as an investment account or a house that is held in the name of only one party) also would be nonmarital property. In some states, however, the increase in value would be marital property.

MARITAL OR COMMUNITY PROPERTY

Marital or **community property** is defined somewhat differently by different states, but it generally includes property and income acquired during the marriage. Wages earned during the marriage are marital property. A home and furniture purchased during the marriage usually are considered marital property.

When property is considered to be marital or community property, the court has the power to divide the property between the parties. Unlike separate or nonmarital property, one party does not have an automatic right to keep the property in the event of a divorce.

If title to property is held in the name of only one spouse, that does not necessarily mean that the property is not marital or community property. Assume, for example, that wife and husband both work and use their wages to purchase a car. If title to the car is only in the wife's name or only in the husband's name, the car still is marital property because payments for the car came from marital funds (their wages). Even if one spouse bought the car with his or her wages, was the only driver, and held title to the car, the car still is marital property because payments came from marital funds.

As a practical matter, if husband and wife owned two cars and a judge had to decide who receives which car, the husband and wife probably would each receive the vehicle that he or she primarily drove. Nonetheless, if the property in question is marital property, the judge has the power to give it to either party.

A pension also is usually marital property, even though it may have been earned by the labor of only one spouse during the marriage. To the extent that rights to a pension were earned partially during the marriage and partially during a period when the parties were not married, the part earned during the marriage may be marital property and the part earned when the parties were not married may be nonmarital property. (A later section in this chapter [pages 83 to 86] discusses pensions in more detail.)

DIVIDING MARITAL OR COMMUNITY PROPERTY

A few states, such as California, take a rather simple approach. Lawmakers in those states believe property should be divided equally because they view marriage as a joint undertaking in which both spouses are presumed to contribute equally to the acquisition and preservation of property. The contributions may be different in nature, but they are treated equally. The wage earner does not receive more property than the homemaker, and vice versa. All marital property will be divided fifty-fifty, unless the husband and wife had a premarital agreement stating otherwise. (Premarital agreements are discussed in chapter 2.)

The California community property approach saves resources. Husbands and wives do not have to spend time and money arguing about who should receive more property, since the law of that state already has determined that community property will be divided fifty-fifty. (In California, there still may be issues to dispute, such as: What is and what is not community property? What is the value of a particular piece of community property? For example, if an actress divorces midway in production of a film, how does one value her interest in the film?)

Although California may save resources by declaring an automatic fifty-fifty split, it deprives courts of the opportunity to fine-tune property divisions to meet the needs of individual cases. In several other community property states and in all **equitable distribution states**, courts are allowed to fine-tune property divisions. (That may or may not be an advantage, depending on the cost of fighting over what is "equitable" and one's faith in judges to make fair decisions regarding property.)

"Equitable distribution" means a court divides marital property as it thinks is fair. Like community property states, states applying principles of equitable distribution view marriage as a shared enterprise in which both spouses usually contribute significantly to the acquisition and preservation of property. Unlike the community property approach of California, however, equitable distribution states are not locked into a fifty-fifty split. The division of property could be fifty-fifty, sixty-forty, seventy-thirty, or even all for one spouse and nothing for the other (although that would be very unusual). Under equitable distribution, courts consider a variety of factors and need not weigh the factors equally. That permits more flexibility and more attention to the financial situation of both spouses after the divorce. However, it also makes the resolution of property issues less predictable.

Here are some of the factors that are generally considered by states applying principles of equitable distribution:

1. **Nonmarital Property.** If one spouse has significantly more nonmarital property than the other, that could be a basis for giving more marital property to the less wealthy spouse. As noted, courts are not obliged to give equal amounts of property to each spouse, but if the parties have sufficient assets to leave each party in a comfortable situation after the divorce, courts usually will try to do so.

2. **Earning Power.** If one spouse has more earning power than the other, that could be a basis for giving more marital property to the spouse with less earning power. Courts reason that the party with greater earning power can regain money lost in a divorce more easily than the party with less earning power.

3. **Who Earned the Property.** That can be a factor in favor of the party who worked hard to acquire or maintain the property. When courts apply this factor to a family business, it is common for a court to award all the interest, or a majority of the interest, in the family business to the spouse who operates the business. In that circumstance, the court not only is considering who earned the property,

but also is seeking to disentangle the husband and wife from each other's future financial affairs. If the value of the business is approximately the same as the value of the family home, it is common for the court to give the business to the spouse who primarily operates the business and give the home to the other spouse.

4. Services as a Homemaker. Courts recognize that keeping a home and raising children are work. In addition, those services often enable the spouse who is working outside the home to earn more money. Thus, services as a homemaker are a factor in favor of the homemaker. Some courts also apply a related concept of considering whether one spouse had impaired his or her earning capacity because of working as a homemaker. If a party can show his or her work as a homemaker resulted in missing the opportunity for training or job experience that could have resulted in higher income, that factor can favor giving more property to the homemaker-spouse.

5. Waste and Dissipation. If a spouse wasted money during the marriage, that could count against him or her when it comes time to divide property. This factor is sometimes labeled **economic fault**, and may be considered even by courts that do not consider other kinds of fault. Waste or dissipation could include gambling losses, significant sums of money given away to family members (particularly over the protest of the other spouse), and money spent on pursuing romantic relationships outside the marriage. Business losses occasionally are considered waste or dissipation, but more often they are considered an ordinary risk for which neither spouse should be penalized (particularly if the business deal would have benefited both parties had it gone better). In some states, before waste or dissipation can be a factor, it must be shown that the waste or dissipation occurred when the marriage was breaking down (a relatively short time before or after one spouse filed for divorce). In other states, waste or dissipation at any time during the marriage could be relevant.

6. Fault. Noneconomic fault, such as spousal abuse or marital infidelity, is considered in some states, but most states do not consider it relevant to property division. In years past (particularly prior to 1970), one needed to show fault by the other party in order to obtain a divorce, and fault was an important consideration in dividing property and setting support. Over time, however, most courts and legislatures concluded that it was too difficult and not worth the time to try to sort out all the transgressions that may have occurred in a marriage, particularly when many of them are of a subjective nature. The more modern view is that courts should focus primarily on economic factors when dividing property and pay less attention to who did what to whom.

7. Duration of Marriage. A long marriage may be a factor in favor of a larger property award to the spouse with less wealth or earning power. The longer the marriage, the more likely a court is to view the husband and wife as equal partners.

8. Age and Health of Parties. If one spouse has ill health or is significantly older than the other, that factor could favor a larger award to the sicker or older spouse. When the factor is mentioned by a court, it most often is in connection with an older wife whose ability to earn money is diminished by her age and health. The factor can apply to men too, particularly if the man is of an age at which it is not reasonable to assume that he can go out and re-earn a substantial amount of assets if his wife were given a majority of the marital assets. In such a case, an equal division of assets would be more likely.

9. Tax Consequences. The tax consequences of property division can be considered when dividing property. If, for example, the sale of a house or the sale of stock in a company as part of a divorce will result in payment of capital gains tax, the court can consider that when dividing the property. The person who will have to pay the tax may receive some extra property to compensate for the added tax he or she will have to pay. Conversely, if a property settlement results in a tax benefit, the person receiving the benefit may receive less property because of that benefit. In order for a court to consider tax consequences, the consequences usually must be immediate and specific. The court generally does not want to speculate about possible tax consequences that may occur several years in the future.

10. Premarital Agreements. A written premarital agreement, assuming it is valid, can be a trump card in dividing marital property.

By entering into a premarital agreement, the wife and husband have agreed to waive their rights to have a court consider the usual cluster of factors in dividing property. Instead, the parties through their agreement have determined in advance how their property should be divided in the event of a divorce. (For more information about premarital agreements, see chapter 2.)

THE FAMILY HOME

If the wife and husband can agree between themselves on what should happen to the home, the court virtually always will accept their decision. If the wife and husband cannot agree, the court will decide.

If the parties own a house, condominium, or cooperative apartment and they have children who are still living at home, the law favors giving the house to the spouse who will have primary custody of the children, if it is affordable to do so. This promotes continuity in the lives of the children as well as in the life of the spouse who will live in the house.

If the parties cannot afford to keep the house, it may be sold and the proceeds divided (or perhaps given to one party). Division of money from sale of the house generally is made after paying off the mortgage and the costs of the sale such as commissions to the real estate brokers, transfer tax, and attorneys' fees.

In some cases, there is a middle-ground approach: The spouse who has primary custody of the children will have a right to live in the house for a certain number of years, such as until the youngest child graduates high school. At the end of that time, that spouse will buy out the other spouse's interest or sell the house and divide the proceeds.

A variation on these arrangements is to give one spouse a right to buy out the other spouse for a fixed period of time, such as thirty days. If the first spouse cannot buy out the other spouse (perhaps because he or she was not able to obtain financing), then the second spouse has an equal period of time to buy out the first spouse. If neither spouse is able to buy out the other, then the house will be sold and the proceeds divided.

When only one spouse is going to occupy the house after a divorce, arrangements need to be made for payment of expenses related to the house. A common arrangement is for the party living in the house to pay the mortgage, property taxes, utilities, and routine repairs. If the spouse who is not living in the house retains an interest in the house (such as a right to share in the proceeds when the house is sold at a later date), both parties might share in the costs of major repairs. Major repairs might be defined by the nature of the expense (repair of roof, replacement of appliance) or by dollar amount—for example, any repair costing more than $200.

In some cases, the monetary interest of the spouse who is not living in the house may be set at a fixed dollar amount. That amount could be adjusted for inflation based on the Consumer Price Index (issued by the U.S. Department of Commerce, Bureau of Labor Statistics) or by the percent increase in the value of the house from the date of the divorce to the date of sale of the house.

Here is an example of the second situation. Assume that a house is determined to be worth $150,000 at the time of divorce in 1996 and that the spouse who moved out was given a $30,000 interest in the house at the time of divorce. If the house is sold ten years later for $300,000, the spouse who originally was given a $30,000 interest in the house would then receive $60,000, since the value of the house doubled between the time of divorce and the time of sale.

When a court or a marital settlement agreement gives the entire interest in the house to one spouse and makes that spouse responsible for paying future mortgage payments, that does not mean the spouse who moves out is no longer potentially liable for the mortgage. Banks and other lending institutions are very reluctant to give up the security of having more than one person responsible for the loan. The spouse who moved out still is responsible for the loan in the event the other spouse does not pay the mortgage.

The legal remedy for the spouse who moved out is a **hold harmless provision**. That means that if the spouse who moved out is obliged to pay a loan that the other spouse was supposed to pay, then the spouse who moved out can collect the loss from the spouse who has the house. The spouse who moved out can sue his or her former partner for any lost funds. Assuming the house has a positive net worth, the court could order the house sold in order to pay back the spouse who moved out.

FAMILY-OWNED BUSINESS
(AND WAYS TO FIND HIDDEN MONEY)

As noted in the section on dividing marital and community property, courts usually favor giving a family-owned business to the spouse who runs the business. The other spouse may be given other assets in exchange, such as the family home or bank accounts.

The situation is more complicated if both wife and husband have been actively involved in the business. The court may set up an arrangement by which one spouse has the right to buy out the other spouse over time. Alternatively, the right to buy out the other could be sequential—first given to one spouse for a certain period of time, then to the other spouse for the same period of time. As with handling division of the family home, a forced sale might be an option if neither party can buy out the other party (although most courts would favor giving the business to just one spouse rather than dissolving an ongoing business).

If the court thinks the parties can continue to work together despite the divorce, the court may continue the *status quo* with the husband and wife remaining as business partners, even though they are no longer marital partners.

Valuation of family businesses can be tricky. A **closely held business** does not have a value that can be readily ascertained on a stock exchange. If the business is of sufficient size, it could be worth the parties' efforts to hire experts such as accountants to evaluate the business, assuming the value of the business is disputed or uncertain. On the other hand, if the business is very small or clearly does not have a significant positive value, it probably will not be worth the time and money to thoroughly evaluate the business.

When trying to ascertain the value of a business, it is helpful to look at financial statements of the business, reflecting the business's assets, liabilities, income, and expenses. Tax returns and checking account records also can provide valuable information—sometimes more accurate than the company's internal financial statements.

Loan applications of the business (or of the owner of the business) may provide highly valuable information. Businesses and individuals may make "generous" statements about income and assets when seeking a loan. That can be useful for obtaining a loan. It also is very useful to the spouse of the business owner when the spouse wants to show that the business is worth more than the business owner claims when divorce is at issue.

If there has been a recent good faith offer to buy the business, that, of course, is valuable evidence about the value of the business. In addition, if there is information available about the purchase price of similar businesses, that too is useful.

Businesses whose customers usually pay in cash can be particularly hard to value, especially if the owner tries to hide income. If the stated income of the business owner does not match the amount of money the parties have been spending over the past few years, proof of the parties' expenses compared with declared income can create an inference to the court that the business is worth more than the owner says it is.

Another source of information about a closely held business may be a disgruntled former (or current) employee of the business. An employee unhappy with the boss may be willing to pass on information about how much money really is made and what the expenses are.

If the spouse who is not the business owner presents proof about hidden income or inflated expenses, that can be the basis for a greater award of other property, as well as perhaps higher alimony and child support. When seeking to claim that income is greater than what the other party says it is, one needs to be alert for other explanations for the added funds. If the business owner has been meeting family expenses with loans that have to be repaid, the funds from those loans would not be a basis for a larger award of property, alimony, or child support to the other spouse. Instead, the other spouse may receive a lesser amount of property, alimony, and child support, since the business owner is likely to be saddled with the debt that needs to be repaid.

LOOKING FOR HIDDEN ASSETS

In addition to the financial records discussed in this section, consider checking the following items in cases where the other party is suspected of hiding income and assets:

- **Original tax returns.** If you have reason to believe that the tax returns given to you or your attorney are not the actual returns filed with the Internal Revenue Service (or state tax department), fill out a form requesting the Internal Revenue Service to send you a copy of the original. Your spouse's signature may be required if you did not sign the tax return. A court can require that your spouse provide his or her signature.

- **Children's bank accounts.** A child's bank account might be a hiding place for money. A trace on the source of those assets could lead to discovery of more income and assets. Similarly, joint bank accounts held by a spouse and another relative also could be a hiding place for income and assets.

- **Safety deposit boxes.** Find out (perhaps through court-ordered discovery) where your spouse has safety deposit boxes. Check the bank records for access to the box and see if the times of access coincide with other significant events.

- **Manipulation of expenses, perks, and income.** The owner of a closely held business often can manipulate expenses, perks, and income to make it appear he or she has less income or assets at the time of a divorce. If these items have shifted significantly near the time of divorce, further comparisons and inquiries are warranted.

PENSIONS

When a couple divorces, they probably focus first on dividing up the property that's easy to see—the home, furniture, cars, and so on. The property they can't see—their **intangible property**—is also affected by divorce. Pensions are one kind of intangible property. For many families, a pension is the largest asset, after the family home. Even if the pension is earned solely by the efforts of one spouse, the portion of it that was earned during the marriage is still marital property subject to division by the court. (For discussion of how a pension can be considered nonmarital and marital, see the earlier section on "Marital or Community Property," pages 74 to 75.)

Many courts prefer to give full rights to a pension to the party who earned it as long as the other party will have a sufficient amount of income and property from other sources.

SOCIAL SECURITY BENEFITS

Divorced spouses also may be eligible to collect Social Security retirement benefits based on their ex-spouse's work record. The divorced spouse is generally eligible to collect benefits if the divorced spouse:

- is sixty-two or older,
- is unmarried,
- was married to the worker for at least ten years, and
- is not entitled to benefits, on own or other account, that exceed one-half the worker's primary benefit amount.

The wage-earning spouse doesn't have to be retired and actually drawing benefits; he or she just has to be eligible for retirement benefits.

The impact of divorce on Social Security retirement benefits is very different from its impact on pension benefits. A worker with a pension is eligible for a certain amount of money in benefits. If a court orders these benefits split between the parties, the worker's share will go down.

With Social Security retirement benefits, the eligibility of a divorced spouse has no effect on the amount the worker is entitled to. The worker will collect that amount whether he or she has no eligible spouse, an eligible ex-spouse, or even four ex-spouses all eligible to collect based on his or her work record.

If, however, the pension is the primary source of income that a spouse would have and there are no other significant sources of income, the court is likely to divide rights to the pension. The court can divide the pension between the spouses by percentages (e.g., one spouse will receive 60 percent, the other spouse, 40 percent) or by a fixed cash amount to one spouse with the remainder to the other spouse (e.g., one spouse will get $600 per month, the other spouse, $400).

Congress has passed a law facilitating division of pensions. The law allows entry of orders by a court called **Qualified Domestic Relations Orders (QDROs)**. These orders, when properly entered by a

That's one reason establishing eligibility for a divorced spouse is normally not difficult. It doesn't require a court appearance or even notification to the worker. It simply requires presenting the appropriate documentation to the Social Security Administration. Documentation would normally include proof of:

- identity,
- each party's age and Social Security number,
- marriage, and
- divorce (must be a complete divorce, not a separation or an annulment).

Generally, original documents are best, but certified copies will do.

A divorced spouse also may be eligible for benefits on the account of a deceased wage earner if the wage earner would have been eligible for benefits if alive. Requirements are similar to those outlined above, except that the surviving divorced spouse must be at least sixty (or at least fifty and disabled or be caring for a child who is also eligible to receive benefits on the deceased wage earner's account). The surviving divorced spouse can remarry without loss of benefits after age sixty (age fifty if disabled). The amount of the benefit is approximately equal to the wage earner's primary benefit amount. As with retirement benefits, more than one person can collect. Applicants will need the documents outlined above, along with proof of the wage earner's death and, if applicable, of disability.

court, require the administrator of a pension plan to send pension checks not only to the worker, but also to the worker's former spouse. The court cannot order a pension check to be written before the worker is entitled to the pension, nor can the court change the total amount of the pension that is due. But the court can direct that when a worker is eligible for a pension (even if he or she has not yet retired and is not drawing a pension), checks must be sent to the worker's former spouse.

For example, if a couple is divorcing after a worker has retired, the court may order that pension payments be divided fifty-fifty (or by some other percentage). If the couple divorces while the worker is still employed and accumulating retirement benefits, the court may ascertain the value of the pension as of the date of the divorce and order division of that sum. When the worker later becomes eligible for payment of retirement benefits, the spouse could receive pension payments for a portion of the pension earned during the marriage. The worker would receive the remainder of the pension, including all of the pension that accumulated after the divorce.

Qualified Domestic Relations Orders can be applied to pensions of most private employers. If a spouse has a military pension or certain types of government pensions, different types of orders with different types of forms may be required, but in most cases, the result can be the same: With a properly entered order by a court, the pension can be divided between the spouses.

DIVIDING PERSONAL PROPERTY

Even in contested cases that have to be decided by a judge, most parties manage to decide between themselves how to divide the relatively small items of personal property. Nonetheless, the phrase "they battled down to who got the last teaspoon" reflects the intensity of emotion that can come with divorce.

Even couples who are relatively amicable when splitting up usually manage to find a few pieces of property to fight over. The individual piece of property often is not truly important by itself, but it comes to represent the frustrations of a relationship that has failed. Perhaps it is easier to obtain an emotional release from fighting over some object than focusing on the underlying personal characteristics that caused the marriage to end.

If the parties truly cannot resolve a dispute over personal property, a judge can do it for them, but that normally is not a cost-effective way to resolve the issue. If the judge does have to resolve the dispute, the judge will consider the same factors discussed earlier in the section on dividing marital or community property (pages 75 to 79). In addition, the judge may consider who acquired the property, who uses the property, and whether the property has a special connection to the original family of one spouse.

If the wife and husband are having a difficult time dividing personal property, they might try some techniques that have been used by other couples.

The spouses together can prepare a list of all the property in dispute. One spouse can take that list and divide it into two separate lists. Then the other spouse can choose which of the two lists to take as his or her property. Presumably, the spouse who drew up the two lists will have an incentive to prepare an equal division of property. This arrangement is a variation on the way parents often encourage children to divide a disputed candy bar: Have one child divide the candy bar and let the other child choose which piece to take.

Another option is to use a single list of disputed property. By flip of a coin or other method, one spouse chooses the first piece of property; then the other chooses; and back and forth it goes until all the property is divided. A variation on this approach would be to have a series of lists from which the spouses take turns, one list at a time. The lists might be categorized by the economic value or sentimental value of the items on each list.

Another somewhat elaborate approach could be used if the parties decide on an unequal division of property but have not decided how to allocate the property. This approach also can be used for equal divisions of property. Again, the parties draw up a list of disputed property. Then they must agree on the value of each item of property, and post the value next to the item. The parties take turns selecting items of property. When either the husband or the wife has reached his or her designated quota (for example, 65 percent of the property as determined by the agreed values), then the other party receives the rest of the property.

If the husband and wife have difficulty agreeing on the value of personal property, they might hire a neutral property appraiser to set values of the property. Appraisers often can be found in the Yellow Pages under "Appraisers" or "Estate Sales."

PERSONAL INJURY AWARDS

Occasionally couples are faced with dividing a personal injury damage award. If, for example, the husband or wife were involved in an auto accident for which someone else was at fault, the party who was injured might receive (or be entitled to receive in the future) a sum of money for the damages. When the couple divorces, who is entitled to the damage award?

States take different approaches to the issue. Some states view the award as separate or nonmarital property. Thus, all of the damage award belongs to the injured party. Courts in those states reason that the injury was suffered by only one spouse, and the damage award was designed to make the injured spouse whole. Therefore, all of the damage award belongs to the injured spouse.

In some personal injury lawsuits, there are two damage awards: one for the spouse who received the physical injury and another damage award for the spouse of the injured party to compensate that spouse for loss of companionship, or **consortium**, that resulted from the injury. (Loss of consortium refers to loss of sexual relations and, under some definitions, the term also refers to loss of general companionship.) If a state treated damage awards as separate or nonmarital property, each spouse would be entitled to his or her own damage award, but they would not be entitled to any portion of their partner's award.

Other states treat damage awards as marital or community property, which means the court can divide the award between the husband and wife. Courts in these states reason that the damage award arose from something that occurred during the marriage and was going to benefit the entire family; therefore, the award should be treated as marital property. In practice, courts in these states are likely to give more of the damage award to the injured party, but the court has the power to allocate some of the award to the other spouse.

In other states, there is mid-ground approach that focuses on the type of damage award. Many personal injury damage awards (particularly those set by a judge or jury) are divided into parts. Depending on what type of damage award is given, the payment may go to the injured party or to the parties jointly. Payments for medical expenses are likely to go to whichever party will pay the medical bills; payments for pain and suffering are likely to go to the injured party who experienced the pain and suffering; and payments for lost wages may go to both parties, since the wages would have benefited them both.

ALLOCATION OF DEBTS

In addition to dividing property, most couples also have debts to divide. Sometimes the debts will exceed the assets. The court, or the parties by agreement, will divide whatever property the couple has

LOTTERY WINNINGS

As a majority of states have caught "lottery fever," there are a growing number of news stories and court opinions about how lottery winnings are to be divided in the event of a divorce. Sometimes the issue arises when one spouse won a big lottery after the couple has separated but before a divorce is final. The spouse who bought the lottery ticket wants to keep all the winnings for himself or herself, while the other spouse wants a piece of the action.

The rule in most states is that if the winnings came from a lottery ticket purchased during the marriage—even if the parties were separated—the winnings are marital or community property, which means the winnings can be divided between the husband and wife.

and then allocate the responsibility of each party to pay off particular debts. (The wife pays off MasterCard; husband pays off Visa, and so on.)

If the debts were jointly incurred, both parties remain ultimately responsible for them. If the spouse who was supposed to pay a particular bill does not, the creditor still can look to the other spouse to collect the amount due. For example, if during the marriage the husband and wife applied together for a MasterCard, both signing the application and both promising to make payments, both are liable to MasterCard, even if only one spouse made the charges.

If a court or a settlement agreement requires a wife to pay the MasterCard bill, but she does not and MasterCard collects from the husband, the husband can sue the wife for the loss, or he may be able to deduct his loss from future payments he may owe his wife (such as alimony, if there is any).

Given the potential for continued joint debts, even after a divorce, it is important to limit one's liability for the other spouse's debts. Thus, it is best to close joint credit card accounts or other joint accounts as soon as a divorce is pending (unless the party has a great deal of faith in one's soon-to-be ex-spouse). If it is not possible to close an account because there is an outstanding debt that cannot be paid off immediately, it is prudent for a spouse to notify the creditor that he or she will not be responsible for any additional debts beyond current outstanding balances.

For example, if there is an outstanding home equity loan of $10,000, but an available line of credit of $40,000, it probably is best to notify the creditor (orally and in writing) that the line of credit should not be extended beyond $10,000. Similarly, if one spouse co-signed on a business loan for the benefit of the other spouse's business, it would be prudent for the spouse who does not own the business to notify the creditor that he or she will not be responsible for any business debts beyond those already incurred.

One spouse normally will not be responsible for the debts of another spouse if debts were incurred only in the name of the spouse who made the purchase. In many states, however, an exception will be made for debts that are considered family expenses. Examples of family expenses include groceries for the family, the children's necessary medical expenses, and children's clothes. If a debt is considered to be a family expense, both spouses probably are liable for the debt, even if only one of them incurred the debt. Community property states also generally make spouses liable for each other's debts incurred during the marriage.

Educational loans are a common debt. Generally, a court will direct each party to repay his or her own loans for educational expenses. If, however, the debts were incurred during the marriage, it is possible for the court to direct one spouse to repay the other spouse's educational debts.

MODIFYING OR UNDOING A PROPERTY DIVISION

A property division agreed to by the parties or ordered by the court is very hard to get out of. Courts favor "done deals" and do not want to encourage the parties to run back to court to litigate their dispute all over again.

In most states, there is a period of time after a court enters its order during which one of the parties can ask the court to reconsider its decision. Such a request may be called a **motion to reconsider** or a **motion to vacate the judgment**. The time period for making such a request varies among states, but it is often thirty days after entry of the court's order that is at issue.

The party seeking reconsideration may argue that the court made a mistake in understanding the facts of the case or in applying the law. The party also may claim that some new facts have arisen that make the original order unfair. (Generally, the party claiming new facts must have a good reason for not having discovered the facts earlier.) In most cases, courts turn down a party's request for reconsideration, but if the court accepts the party's arguments, the court may modify the order or conduct additional hearings.

Fraud or **duress** are two other bases for seeking modification of a court order or settlement agreement. Fraud means that one party has deliberately deceived the other party on a significant matter. If, for example, one party to a settlement agreement lied about the amount of his or her assets and the other party later found out that a substantial amount of assets were hidden, that could be a basis for asking the court to vacate the property settlement and order a new distribution of property.

Duress occurs when one party is forced into an agreement by extreme, unfair pressure from the other party. In this circumstance, a court also might vacate an agreement and order a different distribution of property. Duress is difficult to prove. Most judges assume that parties to a divorce agreement are under some degree of stress. The amount of stress and pressure that a party must have been under before a court will allow the party to back out of a deal is very high.

The time period for seeking to modify an agreement or order on the basis of fraud or duress usually is longer than the time period for asking for reconsideration because of the court's mistake of facts or law. The time period varies from state to state, but a period of one year from the time of the order or agreement is common.

If a party does not like a trial court's decision, another way to seek relief is to appeal to a higher court. The first appeal usually is to the state's appellate court, although if the case has been decided in a small state or if the case involves an issue of substantial public importance, a direct appeal to the state's supreme court may be possible.

Appeals are expensive—often costing as much as the cost of the trial. The decision to appeal must be made promptly, often within thirty days of the trial court's decision. If the party wanting to appeal waits beyond the period provided by statute or court rule for filing a **notice of appeal**, the right to appeal may be lost. The notice of appeal is a document that lets the trial court, the appellate court, and the opposing party know that an appeal will be taken.

More appeals are unsuccessful than successful. The likelihood of success depends on the facts of the case. Before taking an appeal, a party may wish to seek an outside opinion from an attorney who has not been connected with the case regarding the likelihood of success of the appeal. Sometimes the attorney who handled the trial has been so close to the case that he or she cannot be fully objective about the merits of an appeal.

EFFECT OF BANKRUPTCY

A property settlement might be dischargeable in bankruptcy or it might not be dischargeable, depending on the facts of the case. A **discharge in bankruptcy** means that all of a debt or a portion of a debt no longer has to be paid, because a federal court has declared the debtor to be bankrupt.

Prior to 1994, many former spouses of persons who declared bankruptcy after the divorce found themselves out of luck when seeking to collect what was due. A wife, for example, may have agreed to a divorce based on a promise from her husband that three years after the divorce, he would pay her a certain amount of money as part of the property settlement. If after the divorce was finalized, the husband declared bankruptcy, the wife might never collect the amount that was due.

Congress saw the potential unfairness of this, particularly in cases in which the debtor is technically bankrupt (owing more money than the debtor has assets), but the debtor nonetheless still has the capacity to pay many debts. The new law, which took effect in 1994, allows the bankruptcy court to weigh the hardships between the parties. If it appears that the bankrupt debtor has enough property and income to pay the debt to the ex-spouse, the debtor will have to do so. If the debtor truly does not have enough money for basic support of the debtor and his or her dependents, then all or a portion of the debt may be discharged in bankruptcy.

Although in appropriate circumstances, a bankruptcy court has the power to discharge a debt owed in a property settlement, the court cannot discharge past-due payments for alimony or child support. A debtor's bankruptcy may be a basis for reducing *future* alimony and child support, but not for reducing or eliminating *past-due* alimony and child support.

CHAPTER TEN

■

Alimony/Maintenance

"ALIMONY" AND "MAINTENANCE" are terms that refer to payments from one spouse to the other spouse for the benefit of the spouse who is receiving payment. Some states use the term **alimony**; other states use the term **maintenance**; both mean the same thing. Only about 15 percent of divorces or separations involve payments of alimony. (For simplification in the rest of this section, we will use only the term "alimony," but wherever "alimony" is used, "maintenance" could be substituted.)

The overwhelming majority of alimony awards are from the husband to the wife, but in appropriate circumstances (such as a husband who takes care of the children and home while the wife works outside the home), payments from the wife to the husband also can be ordered. The United States Supreme Court has held that it is unconstitutional for a state's statute to allow alimony payments only to the wife; if payments to the wife are permitted, payments to the husband must be permissible too. All states allow courts to order alimony. (For many years, Texas laws prohibited courts from ordering alimony, but those laws have been repealed.)

There are several types of alimony, each of which is designed to meet particular needs.

TEMPORARY ALIMONY

Temporary alimony or **alimony pendente lite** is alimony given when the parties are separated but the divorce is not final. "Pendente lite" is a Latin phrase meaning "pending the suit." Alimony may be continued under a different label after the divorce is final, but it need not be.

REHABILITATIVE ALIMONY

Rehabilitative alimony refers to alimony that is given to a spouse so that the spouse may "rehabilitate" herself or himself in the sense of acquiring greater earning power or training in order to become self-supporting. Rehabilitative alimony also might be given to a parent who is staying home with young children until such time as it is considered appropriate for the parent to work outside the home.

There is no uniform time at which parents automatically are expected to work outside the home, but when the youngest child is in school full-time is a common time for the parent to resume work. (Of course, in many families, intact and divorced, the parents work outside the home when the children are preschoolers. And in some families, one parent stays home as long as the children live at home.)

Rehabilitative alimony is usually for a fixed period of time. The court (or the parties by agreement) may include a provision that the alimony is subject to **review** at the end of that period. If alimony is subject to review, it means the court may look at the facts of a case at a later time to determine whether alimony should be continued, discontinued, or changed in amount.

If the order or agreement regarding alimony does not contain a provision for review, it might still be reviewable, or it might not be reviewable, depending on the law of the state. If the recipient of alimony wants the alimony to be reviewable (with the possibility of continuation), it is best to include language to that effect. If the payor of alimony does not want alimony to be continued beyond a certain time, the payor should seek to have language to that effect in the agreement or order. A court is likely to approve cessation of alimony on a certain date if that is what the agreement or order calls for, but the court usually has the power to continue alimony in certain circumstances, such as chronic illness of the recipient.

PERMANENT ALIMONY

Permanent alimony continues indefinitely. The main bases for ceasing payments of permanent alimony are the death of the payor, the death of the recipient, or the remarriage of the recipient. Cohabitation of the recipient with a member of the opposite sex also is a common basis for cessation of permanent alimony. Generally, the cohabitation needs to be of a permanent or near-permanent nature, with the parties who are living together sharing living expenses. A few overnight visits usually do not constitute cohabitation for the purpose of stopping alimony payments.

Unless an agreement between the parties says otherwise, payments of permanent alimony can be adjusted upward or downward based on a change of circumstances. If the recipient gains employment at a well-paying job or receives a significant amount of money from another source, that might be a basis for reducing alimony payments. If the recipient incurs unexpected medical expenses (that are not covered by insurance), that might be a basis for increasing alimony payments, if the spouse paying alimony has the ability to pay more.

A drop in income by the payor, including at retirement, can be a basis for reducing alimony. Courts may examine the reason for a drop in income, and if the drop in income of the payor is in good faith or not through the fault of the payor, the court is more likely to approve a reduction in alimony. If the drop in income seems to have been engineered by the payor to create a basis for reducing alimony, the court is more likely to disapprove a reduction in alimony.

REIMBURSEMENT ALIMONY

Reimbursement alimony, as the name implies, is designed to reimburse one spouse for expenses incurred by the other. If, for example, one spouse helped put the other spouse through college or a training program and the couple divorces soon after the training program is complete, the spouse who supported the family during that period might be able to obtain reimbursement alimony as a payback for the resources spent.

A classic example is the nurse who marries a medical student and supports the family while the medical student finishes medical school (and perhaps a residency program). If the couple divorces soon after the medical student completed training, the nurse probably would be entitled to reimbursement alimony to compensate for the resources used during the training program. In this case, reimbursement alimony is not necessarily being given because the nurse needs funds for day-to-day support (since the nurse would seem to be self-supporting). Instead, the alimony is given as an equitable payback for supporting the spouse through medical school.

Alternatively, a court could choose to give the supporting spouse a substantial majority of marital property in compensation. But in many cases in which one spouse has just completed a training program, the couple has not accumulated a large amount of marital assets. So reimbursement alimony is given as an alternative. Reimbursement alimony can be paid over a period of time.

TAX ASPECTS OF ALIMONY

Alimony usually is treated as income to the recipient and a deduction from income to the person paying alimony. This can result in a savings in the combined income tax payments of the husband and wife. The reason for the savings is that additional income to the wife (in the form of alimony) will be taxed at a lower rate than if it was treated as income to the husband.

Assume a husband and wife are about to be divorced. Before payment of alimony, the wife has a taxable income of $10,000 and the husband has a taxable income of $70,000. If they each were to pay taxes on these amounts, their combined tax liability would be $18,601. (The husband would pay $17,097; the wife would pay $1,504, applying the 1994 federal tax tables.)

If the husband were to pay the wife $20,000 per year in alimony, his taxable income would drop to $50,000, and the wife's taxable income would increase to $30,000. Their combined federal income tax payments would be $16,500 ($11,050 by husband and $5,450 by wife). The savings on their combined tax bills would be $2,101 over what would be paid if the alimony payments were taxable to the husband.

The wife's tax bills have gone up, but so has her income.

LUMP-SUM ALIMONY

Lump-sum alimony, or **alimony in gross,** refers to alimony that is a fixed payment which generally will be made regardless of circumstances that would be a basis for termination of other types of alimony. For example, lump-sum alimony, or alimony in gross, normally would be paid even if the recipient remarries. Depending on the wording of the agreement or order, payments also could be made to the estate of the recipient in the event the recipient dies.

This type of alimony usually is in lieu of a property settlement. Depending on how the alimony is structured, it could provide a tax advantage to the payor by being deductible to the payor and income to the recipient. Lump-sum alimony, or alimony in gross, could be used as a type of reimbursement alimony to ensure that one spouse is paid back for certain expenditures, even if the recipient remarries, cohabits with someone, or does not otherwise need the alimony for day-to-day support.

CRITERIA FOR ORDERING ALIMONY

The criteria for ordering alimony have been discussed, in part, in the descriptions of different types of alimony. The factors considered by a court when deciding whether to order alimony based on need of the recipient are similar to the factors considered by a court when dividing property. (See pages 75 to 79.)

1. Income and Property of Each Party. The greater the income and property a divorced spouse has, the less likely it is that the spouse will need alimony. Conversely, the less income and property a spouse has, the more she or he will need alimony. Payment of alimony also depends on the ability of one spouse to pay. Alimony is most likely when there is a substantial difference in the property and income of one spouse versus the other. If the spouses' levels of property and income are similar, alimony is less likely. In looking at the difference in property held by the spouses, courts consider the division of property in connection with the divorce. Some courts order a larger share of property to the less prosperous spouse in order to avoid or reduce the need for alimony to the less prosperous spouse.

2. Earning Capacity of Each Spouse. A related factor is the present and future earning capacity of each spouse. If one spouse's earning capacity is much larger than the other spouse's earning capacity, that is a significant factor in favor of payment of alimony. To the extent that the earning capacities of the spouses may come closer together by giving the spouse with lower earnings additional time to pursue training, the court may use that as a factor for granting rehabilitative maintenance.

3. Impairments in Earning Capacity. If a spouse has little or no earning capacity, that is a basis for granting alimony—probably permanent alimony. Common examples of such impairments are advanced age or chronic illness. Some courts will also note that earning capacity may be limited because of the number of years the spouse spent working as a homemaker. During that time, the homemaker-spouse delayed or gave up the opportunity for training or building job skills that could produce a higher income. Meanwhile the other spouse was able to increase earning capacity, in part, because his or her partner was managing the home. In such circumstances, some courts will grant permanent alimony to help make up for the difference in earning potentials.

4. Children at Home. The presence of young children at home is a factor in favor of granting alimony, at least until the children are in school full-time. Even after the children are in school, the court may grant alimony so that the parent who is taking care of the children need work only part-time. This factor is more likely to apply if, during the marriage, one of the parents had been serving as a full-time homemaker. If both parents had been working outside the home during the marriage, the court is more likely to expect the *status quo* to continue. (The Census Bureau reports that approximately 60 percent of mothers with preschool children work outside the home.) As with all types of alimony, a key factor is the ability of the more prosperous spouse to pay. If the better-off spouse has only moderate income, alimony probably will not be ordered, or if it is, the amount will be moderate.

5. Standard of Living During the Marriage. A phrase that was commonly bandied about in connection with divorces of more than thirty years ago was "The wife is entitled to be supported in the style to which she has become accustomed." One does not hear that phrase as much anymore, but the standard of living of the husband and wife during the marriage is a factor to be considered by the court. If the parties have sufficient money to continue the same lifestyle when they are separate as when they were married, the court may grant sufficient alimony (and property) to accomplish that. But the reality in most cases is that the money will not go as far as it did during the marriage, since it costs more to support two households than one. It is to the advantage of the party seeking alimony to present testimony and exhibits reflecting a prosperous lifestyle. Exhibits might include pictures or videos of the family home, possessions, and vacations, perhaps accompanied by copies of receipts and checking account records reflecting the level of the family's expenditures. If the couple's relatively high lifestyle during the marriage was supported, in part, by incurring debt, the court will not expect that one party must continue to incur debt to support the other.

6. Duration of Marriage. The longer the marriage, the greater likelihood of alimony, particularly if there is a significant difference in the earning power of the parties. In short-term marriages, alimony is less likely (unless there are young children at home). Alimony normally will not be granted for a time period that is longer than the marriage, but it is possible in some circumstances, such as the chronic disability of the person seeking support.

7. Contributions of the Spouse Seeking Support to the Education or Career of the Other Spouse. As was discussed in the section on reimbursement alimony (pages 96 to 97), a spouse who helps put the other spouse through school or a training program can use that as a factor to gain alimony, even if the alimony is not necessary for the recipient's day-to-day support. Spouses who actively support their partners' careers, such as through frequent entertaining or through working at no wages in the family business, also can use that as a factor in seeking alimony.

8. Tax Consequences of Property Division and Alimony. If the payor of alimony receives a tax benefit as the result of the property distribution, that can be a factor in favor of alimony. Conversely, if the payor of alimony must pay additional taxes because of the property division, that could be a factor for paying less alimony or no alimony. Alimony generally is deductible to the spouse who is paying it and is treated as income to the spouse who is receiving it (unless the parties agree otherwise). If the husband and wife are in different income brackets, the tax treatment of alimony results in a net savings of tax payments when considering the combined tax payments of the husband and wife. The amount of money the payor will save in taxes by being able to deduct alimony from taxable income will be greater than the amount of additional taxes the recipient will pay on the alimony, which is treated as taxable income (see box on page 97 for example).

9. Fault. In a majority of states, fault is not a factor in deciding whether or not to grant alimony. (See chart on pages 102 to 103.) In those states, the legislatures and courts wish to focus on economic factors in deciding who receives alimony, and if so, how much. As with property division in these states, the courts do not want to get in the middle of trying to determine who is more at fault. Thus, if one spouse had an affair or was considered mean to the other spouse, it will not be a factor in setting alimony. In approximately twenty states, however, fault is a factor. In some of those states, proof of fault by the spouse seeking alimony completely blocks that spouse's claim to alimony. In other states, fault is a factor that can be considered in setting alimony, although the presence of fault by the spouse seeking alimony does not necessarily preclude alimony.

10. Premarital Agreements. As with division of property, a valid premarital agreement can be a trump card that determines the level of alimony that will be paid in the event of divorce. Through the premarital agreement, the parties have entered into a contract by which they waive their rights to have alimony determined by the usual rules of court. (For discussion of premarital agreements, see chapter 2.) In many states, a premarital agreement that gives no alimony or very low alimony to the less wealthy spouse will not be honored if the less wealthy spouse will be left with no reasonable means of support. In that circumstance, the spouse who lacks capacity for self-support is likely to be granted some alimony.

CONSIDERATION OF FAULT IN SETTING ALIMONY

	MARITAL FAULT NOT CONSIDERED	MARITAL FAULT RELEVANT
Alabama		x
Alaska	x	
Arizona	x	
Arkansas	x	
California	x	
Colorado	x	
Connecticut		x
Delaware	x	
D.C.		x
Florida		x
Georgia		x
Hawaii	x	
Idaho		x
Illinois	x	
Indiana	x	
Iowa	x	
Kansas	x	
Kentucky	x	
Louisiana		x
Maine		x
Maryland		x
Massachusetts		x
Michigan		x
Minnesota	x	
Mississippi		x
Missouri		x

LIFE INSURANCE TO GUARANTEE ALIMONY

The recipient of alimony may wish to seek an agreement or court order to guarantee support in the event of the payor's death. The usual method of guaranteeing support is to require the payor to maintain an insurance policy on his or her own life with the recipient as beneficiary. The amount of the policy should be high enough to compensate for the loss of alimony payments.

	MARITAL FAULT NOT CONSIDERED	MARITAL FAULT RELEVANT
Montana	x	
Nebraska	x	
Nevada		x
New Hampshire		x
New Jersey	x	
New Mexico	x	
New York		
North Carolina	x	
North Dakota		x
Ohio	x	
Oklahoma	x	
Oregon	x	
Pennsylvania		x
Rhode Island	x	
South Carolina		x
South Dakota		x
Tennessee		x
Texas	x	
Utah	x	
Vermont	x	
Virginia		x
Washington	x	
West Virginia		x
Wisconsin	x	
Wyoming		x

Source: *ABA Family Law Quarterly.*

In order to ensure that the insurance policy remains in effect, the recipient may seek to require the payor to provide periodic proof that the policy is still in force. This could be accomplished by having the payor provide an annual copy of the policy showing full payment of premiums for the coming year. The recipient also may seek to have a provision in the policy that would require the insurance company to notify the recipient in the event that payments are not made on time.

As an alternative to an insurance policy, the parties might agree that the payor will post a bond or that the payor will guarantee to leave the recipient a certain amount of money by will or by trust in order to ensure continued support. Another option is to have the payor sign a **limited irrevocable assignment of income** from his or her pension plan to guarantee the alimony payment. Such a provision would require that alimony payments be deducted from the payor's pension plan in the event that the payor did not make payments directly.

EFFECT OF BANKRUPTCY ON ALIMONY

Past-due alimony is not dischargeable in bankruptcy. That means if one spouse owes the other spouse alimony but has not paid because of financial hard times, the amount that is past due still must be paid. Although a bankruptcy court can discharge many debts—such as credit card debts, medical debts, and student loans—the court cannot discharge an alimony debt. If a debtor has a severe financial problem (as evidenced by the bankruptcy), that could be a basis for reducing future alimony payments, but not for eliminating or reducing past-due alimony payments.

HEALTH INSURANCE

Direct payment of a former spouse's health insurance normally is not part of an alimony agreement or order, although the recipient certainly may wish to use some of the alimony payments to purchase health insurance if the recipient is not already covered.

When a couple divorces, the health insurance policy covering the family (if there was such a policy) no longer covers both spouses. The policy covers only the spouse who had insurance through work or through an individual policy. Children who were covered under a family policy generally are still covered under the policy after a divorce.

A federal law passed in the 1980s requires most employer-sponsored group health plans to offer divorced spouses of covered workers continued coverage at group rates for as long as three years after the divorce. The divorced spouse of a worker must pay for the coverage, but the coverage is available.

A divorced spouse who wishes to take advantage of this law should act as soon as the divorce is final or as soon as the coverage has been lost. He or she should contact the covered worker's employer (human relations or personnel department) to learn the steps that must be taken, but generally the notification has to be within sixty days of the divorce or loss of coverage. Continued coverage is not automatic. The law provides that the worker's employer must explain the divorced spouse's right to continue coverage within fourteen days of being notified, after which the spouse has no more than sixty days to choose to continue the coverage. The employer will advise what coverage is available, its cost, and when payments must be made, as well as any steps that must be taken to establish eligibility for the health insurance.

Health care reforms under consideration by Congress also may make health insurance easier to obtain.

CHAPTER ELEVEN

■

Child Support

THE STARTING POINT FOR DETERMINING CHILD SUP-
PORT usually is the **guideline** that has been set by the state
legislature or by court rule.

Under federal laws passed in the 1980s, states must establish guidelines for determining child support. The guidelines were required because the federal government believed that the amounts ordered for
child support had been too low and that there was too much variation
in the amounts of support for children in similar circumstances.

DEPARTING FROM SUPPORT GUIDELINES

States vary in the degree to which child support guidelines are specific.
Some guidelines are quite detailed and consider many factors. Courts usually depart from such guidelines only in exceptional cases. Other guidelines
are more general—providing a certain amount of support based on income
of the parent (or parents) and the number of children, but not taking into account a variety of factors that could serve as a basis for increasing or de-
creasing the amount of support. Here are some factors that *might* be a basis
for departing from guidelines:

REASONS FOR GOING ABOVE GUIDELINES

- Child care expenses (especially if unusually high)
- Medical and dental expenses not covered by insurance
- Special educational needs, such as private school, tutoring, speech
  therapy

- Recreational activities such as summer camp, sports teams, and after-school activities
- Income of noncustodial parent's new spouse (which may free funds of the noncustodial parent to pay more child support)
- Voluntary unemployment or underemployment of the noncustodial parent (in which case the court may attribute income to the noncustodial parent in an amount that the court thinks the parent should be making, even though he or she is not)

REASONS FOR GOING BELOW GUIDELINES

- Unusual custody arrangements, such as splitting custody of the children (some with mother; some with father)
- Joint custody arrangements in which the child spends an equal amount of time or a substantial amount of time with each parent
- High cost of transportation for child to visit with noncustodial parent, such as when the parents live in different states
- High income of the custodial parent (particularly if the guidelines do not have a cutoff point at a certain level of income, after which the guidelines do not apply)
- The noncustodial parent's duty to support other families, including a new spouse and child
- The noncustodial parent's debts, particularly if the debts were incurred during the marriage to the spouse or former spouse who is seeking support
- Income of the custodial parent's current spouse (which frees funds of the custodial parent to support the child)
- A need to channel funds to a closely held business (which may help the business grow and provide funds for more child support in the future)
- Property division in connection with a divorce, such as giving the custodial parent a home with a paid-off mortgage or low mortgage
- Significant income of the child, such as from a trust fund received by inheritance

Child support guidelines generally resulted in the desired effect: Child support payments increased by approximately 50 percent and support payments within each state became more uniform. One study showed that the average support order increased from $40 per week to $60 per week after the guidelines took effect.

CHILD SUPPORT GUIDELINES BY STATE

	INCOME SHARES	PERCENT OF INCOME	POST-MAJORITY SUPPORT
Alabama	x		x
Alaska		x	
Arizona	x		
Arkansas		x	
California	x		
Colorado	x		x
Connecticut	x		x
Delaware			
D.C.			
Florida	x		
Georgia		x	
Hawaii			x
Idaho	x		
Illinois		x	x
Indiana	x		x
Iowa	x		
Kansas	x		
Kentucky	x		
Louisiana	x		
Maine	x		
Maryland	x		
Massachusetts			x
Michigan	x		x
Minnesota		x	
Mississippi		x	
Missouri	x		x

Guidelines are formulas that consider the income of the parents, the number of children, and perhaps some other factors. The formulas are based on studies of how much families ordinarily spend for raising children.

Guidelines try to approximate the proportion of parental income

	INCOME SHARES	PERCENT OF INCOME	POST-MAJORITY SUPPORT
Montana			
Nebraska	x		
Nevada		x	x
New Hampshire		x	x
New Jersey	x		
New Mexico	x		
New York		x	
North Carolina	x		
North Dakota		x	
Ohio	x		
Oklahoma	x		
Oregon	x		x
Pennsylvania	x		x
Rhode Island	x		
South Carolina	x		x
South Dakota	x		
Tennessee		x	x
Texas		x	
Utah	x		x
Vermont	x		
Virginia	x		
Washington	x		x
West Virginia			x
Wisconsin		x	
Wyoming	x	x	x

Source: *ABA Family Law Quarterly.*

that would have been spent for child support if the family had not been divided by divorce. Courts plug numbers into the formula and come up with an amount of support that should be paid for the child or children. The guidelines apply equally to children born to married parents and to children born out of wedlock.

Parents can argue that because of special circumstances, a court should order more or less support than the guideline amount. (For a list of factors that might be a basis for going above or below guidelines, see the box on pages 106 to 107.)

DETERMINING PARENTS' INCOMES

When applying guidelines, most states look to the parents' net income, although some states use the parents' gross income. **Gross income** means the parents' income from all sources, including wages and investments, with no deductions for taxes or other expenses. Non-wage benefits a parent receives from an employer might be counted as income. For example, military housing allowances usually are counted as income when determining child support. Use of a company car for personal business might also be counted as income. **Net income** means gross income minus federal and state income taxes, Social Security tax, Medicare tax, and deductions for health insurance. Some states will allow other deductions when determining net income. Additional deductions might include: union dues, mandatory retirement contributions, obligations of support to other families (other than the family whose support is currently at issue), and payment on debts incurred during the marriage which were incurred for the benefit of the family.

For self-employed persons, the determination of income may be complex. Courts will allow deductions of reasonable business expenses before determining net income, but courts may disallow unusually high business expenses and depreciation that reduce income artificially without hurting the parent's cash flow.

Thus, certain expenses that are deductible for tax purposes may not be deductible from income for the purpose of setting child support. For example, if a self-employed parent claimed a large deduction for depreciation of office equipment, the deduction may be quite permissible for the Internal Revenue Service, but it might not be treated as a full deduction from income for the purpose of setting child support, particularly if the office equipment will have a long useful life.

EXAMPLES OF GUIDELINES

The amount of money a parent will have to pay in child support varies from state to state because each state has its own guidelines and judges may differ in their willingness to depart from guidelines.

Generally, there are two types of child support guidelines. One type is based on the income of the person who is supposed to pay child support and the number of children. The other type of guideline is based on the income of *both* parents and number of children. This second type of guideline often is referred to as the **income shares model**.

Illinois is an example of a state with guidelines based on the income of only the parent from whom support is due. This is the Illinois guideline in effect in 1996:

NUMBER OF CHILDREN	PERCENTAGE OF SUPPORTING PARTY'S NET INCOME
1	20 percent
2	25 percent
3	32 percent
4	40 percent
5	45 percent
6 or more	50 percent

Under this guideline, if a noncustodial parent ("supporting party") had a net income of $40,000, the annual level of child support would be $8,000 for one child; $10,000 for two children; $12,800 for three children, and so on.

In the "income shares model," which considers the income of both parents, the court first adds the net incomes (or in some states, the gross incomes) of both parents. Then the court consults a long table—or computer program—which assesses the total obligation of support as a percentage of the combined incomes and the number of children. Generally, the percentage drops as the combined incomes rise, on the assumption that financially well-off parents need to spend a smaller portion of their incomes on their children than parents who are less well-off.

The court multiplies the combined incomes by the percentage figure and obtains a dollar amount that the child or children are considered to need for support. Then the responsibility to pay that support is divided between the parents in proportion to each parent's income.

Here is an example using Colorado's child support schedules. Assume a father and mother have two children and a combined annual gross income of $60,000: $40,000 earned by the father and $20,000 earned by the mother. The schedules put the guideline amount for support at $11,508 per year ($959 per month). Since the father earns two thirds of the parties' combined income, he would pay two thirds of the children's support ($7,672 a year) and the mother would pay one third ($3,836).

If one parent had primary custody of the children, the other probably would make a cash payment to that parent. The parent with primary custody probably would not make a cash payment as such, but would be assumed to be spending that amount on the children. Alternatively, the parents might set up a checking account for the children's expenses, deposit their respective shares into the account, and agree on the type of expenses that could be paid from the account.

EFFECTS OF JOINT CUSTODY

A question often arises on the effect of joint custody on child support. The effect of joint custody will depend on the nature of the joint custody arrangement. If the parents have **joint legal custody** (by which they share making major decisions regarding the child), that by itself will have little effect on child support. If the parents have only joint legal custody, one parent still has primary custody of the child and handles payment of most of the child's day-to-day expenses. The custodial parent's expenses for the child have not been reduced by the joint custody arrangement.

If the parents have **joint physical custody**, with the child spending a substantial amount of time with each parent, and if the parents have approximately equal incomes, it is possible neither parent will have to pay support to the other. The father and mother will pay the child's day-to-day expenses when the child is in their respective homes. The parents, however, will need to coordinate payments on major expenses such as camp, school, clothing, and insurance.

If there is a significant difference in the parents' incomes, the parent with higher income probably will make payments to the other parent or pay more of the child's expenses, but the amount paid probably will be less than the guideline amount because of the joint physical custody arrangement.

CHILD SUPPORT DURING SUMMER VACATIONS

Child support usually must be paid by the noncustodial parent when the child is with the noncustodial parent for summer vacations or long holiday breaks. Courts reason that many major expenses for the benefit of the child—such as rent, mortgage, utilities, clothes, and insurance—have to be paid whether the child is with the custodial parent or not. So usually a full support payment is due, even if the child is with the noncustodial parent.

On the other hand, the parties themselves (or the court) are free to set payments in different amounts during vacation periods when the child is with the noncustodial parent. The lower amount for vacation periods with the noncustodial parent might reflect savings to the custodial parent for food expenses or child care.

A related issue may arise if the noncustodial parent wants to reduce child support payments to the custodial parent because the noncustodial parent has spent money on the child, such as for clothes or extracurricular activities. However, that is almost never a basis for reducing child support payments to the custodial parent, unless the parties agreed otherwise.

Court orders or divorce settlements almost always provide that child support is to be paid in specific dollar amounts from one parent to the other. Courts do not want the complications of trying to sort out whether the parties on a particular occasion agreed to an alternative way of making child support payments. Courts also do not want the noncustodial parent unilaterally changing the method of paying child support and potentially interfering with the budget planning of the custodial parent.

If the noncustodial parent wants to pay for clothes or extracurricular activities of the child, that is fine (and nice for the child), but the court will treat such payments as gifts to the child, not as part of the noncustodial parent's support obligation.

COLLEGE EXPENSES

The obligation of a divorced parent to pay for the child's college expenses or trade school will depend on the state in which the parents live and any agreement between the parents regarding such expenses.

Courts in some states will require parents to pay for a child's college expenses, assuming the parents can afford it and the child is a good enough student to benefit from college. Courts in these states reason that the child's parents probably would have helped pay for the child's education had the marriage remained intact and that the child's education should not suffer because of the divorce.

In an Illinois case, for example, the father during the marriage was very enthusiastic about having his son attend his alma mater, Dartmouth College. The father took his son to Dartmouth three times and often bought his son clothes and memorabilia with the Dartmouth logo. The father even arranged for influential alumni of Dartmouth to write letters of recommendation for his son.

After all these efforts, the son got into Dartmouth. But at about that time, the father and mother divorced, and the father no longer wanted to pay for his son to go to Dartmouth. The Illinois courts said that under these circumstances, the father (who earned more than $200,000 per year) had to pay for his son to go to Dartmouth.

In other states, however, a parent's obligation to pay support ceases when the child reaches the age of majority (or graduates high school), and thus the parents are not obliged to pay for the child's college education. Courts in these states note that married parents are not required to pay for their child's college expenses, and therefore divorced parents are not required to do so either.

Regardless of the state's law on compulsory payment of college expenses, the mother and father can agree as part of their divorce settlement to pay for these costs. Courts usually will enforce those agreements.

If parents have earmarked funds earned during the marriage for a child's education, those funds generally would be marital property subject to division between the mother and father by the court. If, however, the funds are in accounts or in savings bonds that have the child's name on them, the funds probably would be viewed as belonging to the child (although one parent may be given the responsibility of managing the funds until the child starts college or reaches adulthood).

Children generally are expected to help pay for their college education and related expenses by working at summer jobs and using some of their own savings. The parents' obligation to pay, if there is such an obligation, will depend on the amount of income and assets of the parents. A parent with low income usually will not be expected to pay for the child's college education.

MODIFICATION OF CHILD SUPPORT

The most common standard for modification of child support is a **substantial change in circumstances**. That usually refers to a change in income of the parent who is supposed to be paying support. If the parent who is obliged to pay support suffers a loss of income, that could be a basis for reducing support; conversely, if the parent's income increases, that could be a basis for increasing support.

Changes in circumstances of the child also can be a reason for modifying support. If the child has significant new expenses, such as orthodonture, special classes, or health needs that are not covered by insurance, that too can be a reason for increasing support.

Significant changes in the income of the parent seeking support also can be a basis for modification. If the custodial parent's income drops (particularly through no fault of the custodial parent), that might be a basis for increasing support. If the custodial parent's income increases, that might be a basis for reducing support from the noncustodial parent.

In some states, support orders may be reviewed automatically every few years to set support consistent with the parents' current income and the support guidelines. If the parent who is supposed to pay support has a major drop in income (such as through loss of a job) and the income is not likely to be replaced soon, the parent should promptly go to court to seek modification of child support.

The obligation to pay support at the designated amount continues until a court orders otherwise. A court's order for child support generally is effective for future support payments only. Normally, a court cannot retroactively modify support payments, even if the parent who was supposed to pay had a good reason for not making full payments.

When a parent loses a job or experiences a financial setback, one of the last things the parent may want to do is incur more expenses by hiring an attorney to try to reduce support. But if the parent has a good reason to reduce support, the money is well spent, since otherwise the support obligation will continue at the original amount. The meter on the cab runs at the same rate, so to speak. As an alternative to an attorney, if the local court is relatively user-friendly, the party seeking to change support might try to represent himself or herself. (For more discussion of representing oneself, see chapter 14.)

REDUCING SUPPORT WHEN CHILD REACHES EIGHTEEN

When a child reaches the age of majority (usually eighteen) or graduates high school, that normally is a basis for stopping child support for that child, unless the parent is obliged to help pay for that child's college education. (For discussion of support for a child's college education, see pages 114 to 115.)

Whether payments stop at age eighteen or at graduation from

high school depends on the law of the state. Many states say payments stop at the later of those two events (assuming the child will graduate high school in a normal amount of time).

If only one child is the subject of a support order, the parent who is obliged to pay child support (the **obligor**) can stop making payments when the child reaches eighteen or graduates high school. The obligor does not have to go to court to seek permission to stop payments.

If there is more than one child who is subject of a support order, the right of the obligor to reduce payments when the oldest child reaches the age of majority will depend on the wording of the court's support order.

If support is set at a certain amount per child (for example, "child support shall be $200 per month for each of the three children"), then the obligor may reduce payments by $200 as each of the three children reach the age of majority. Under this example, child support would be $600 per month when all three children were under eighteen; $400 per month when the oldest child reached eighteen; $200 per month when the middle child reached eighteen; and no support when all three were over eighteen.

If, on the other hand, child support for three children was set as a lump sum for all children (for example "child support for the three children shall be $600 per month"), then the obligor must keep paying $600 per month until the youngest of the three children reaches eighteen, *unless* the obligor goes to court and obtains a reduction in child support.

When the oldest child reaches the age of majority, that can be a basis for a court to reduce support, but it is not an automatic basis for doing so. The court will look at a variety of factors, including the current income of the parents and needs of the remaining children. If the income of the parents has remained the same and the needs of the remaining two minor children are the same, the obligor can expect that the amount of support for the remaining two children will decrease. The amount of reduction will not necessarily be by one third, however. Applying Illinois's child support guidelines (see page 111), for example, the obligor could expect that child support payments would be reduced from 32 percent of his or her net income to 25 percent of net income.

When considering whether to go to court to seek a reduction in child support based on the oldest child reaching majority (or when seeking a reduction on some other basis), the obligor should consider how the guidelines apply to the obligor's *current* income. If the obligor's current income has risen significantly since the last order, a new child support order for two children may actually be more than the guideline amount for three children, since support for three children was set at a time when the obligor's income was lower.

To elaborate on the examples just given, assume that at the time of divorce five years ago an obligor had a net income of $22,500 per year. If the obligor had three children, and Illinois guidelines applied, the obligor would pay 32 percent of net income for child support, which is $7,200 per year or $600 per month. Assume further that the court's order (or the parents' settlement agreement) provided that "child support for the three children shall be $600 per month." Five years later, the obligor's income has doubled (to a net income of $45,000). If the obligor now wants to reduce child support because the oldest child has reached eighteen, the obligor could be in for an unpleasant surprise if he or she went to court.

While it is true that a child's **emancipation** (reaching the age of majority) is a basis for changing child support, the guidelines when applied to the obligor's current income would actually result in an increase in child support. Applying the Illinois guidelines of 25 percent of net income for obligors with two children, support would now be $11,250—a $4,050 per year increase from the old support order even though there is one less child to support.

Similar considerations apply to the parent to whom support is due. If the parent receiving support has had a significant increase in income from wages or elsewhere, that parent may not be able to obtain a significant increase in support if the state's guidelines or other legal principles would shift more of the support obligation to the parent receiving support.

Sometimes it is best not to rush off to court, even though one may be tempted to.

Since the mid-1980s, not a year has gone by without federal and state politicians making proclamations about unpaid child support. The proclamations often are followed up with new laws and regulations designed to improve enforcement and go after "deadbeats." Like the perennial "War on Crime," progress is slow and new laws are not a full solution to the problem.

The Census Bureau reports that only about half of the parents entitled to receive child support receive the full amount that is due. About one quarter of parents to whom support is due receive partial payments, and the other one quarter receive nothing at all. The Census Bureau estimates that each year about $5 billion in court-ordered child support is not paid, making a total unpaid child support debt of about $34 billion as of 1994.

In addition, there are several million mothers who have not obtained orders of child support for their children. A high proportion of those women had children out of wedlock.

For women who actually receive child support, the mean amount is $3,011 per year, or about $250 per month. (These figures are for 1991, the last year in which a complete survey was done. The figures are based on the amount received by each mother without giving a breakdown of how much is paid per child.)

Nonpayment by fathers is not the only child support enforcement problem. In 1995, the Census Bureau reported that the rate at which noncustodial mothers failed to make child support payments is greater than the rate at which noncustodial fathers failed to make child support payments. Thirty-seven percent of noncustodial mothers did not make any court-ordered child support payments, and 24 percent of noncustodial fathers did not make any court-ordered child support payments. Regarding parents who made partial (but not full) court-ordered child support payments, 20 percent of noncustodial mothers and 24 percent of noncustodial fathers made partial payments. Prosecutors who handle support collections estimate that between 2 and 5 percent of their cases involve mothers who did not pay their child support obligations.

Payment of child support correlates with visitation with the child. The Census Bureau reports that eight out of ten fathers with visitation paid child support, and nine out of ten fathers with joint custody paid support. Of the fathers with no visitation rights, fewer than half paid support.

The cost of trying to collect unpaid child support is substantial. According to the U.S. Office of Child Support Enforcement, in Fiscal Year 1993, child support enforcement agencies spent $2.2 billion to collect about $8.9 billion in child support. In other words, each dollar of administrative costs generated about $4 of child support payments (although some portion of child support payments would have been made without involvement of an enforcement agency).

ENFORCEMENT

State and federal governments have a variety of techniques for enforcing payments of child support. The most common is a wage deduction order, by which an employer sends a portion of the obligor-parent's wages to a state agency, which then sends the money to the parent who has custody of the child.

Beginning in 1994, all new child support orders were required to provide for an automatic deduction from the obligor's wages. The wage deduction takes effect immediately unless the parties have

---

EFFECT OF BANKRUPTCY ON CHILD SUPPORT

Bankruptcy's effect on child support is very similar to its effect on alimony, as explained in the box on page 104. Past-due child support is not dischargeable in bankruptcy. If one spouse owes child support but has not paid because of hard times, the past-due amount still must be paid. A bankruptcy court can discharge many debts, but the court cannot discharge a child support debt (or an alimony debt). Severe financial problems (as evidenced by the bankruptcy) could be a basis for reducing future child support payments, but not for reducing past-due payments.

---

agreed otherwise or unless a court waives immediate deductions from wages. Even with such a waiver or agreement, the order must provide that a wage deduction will begin without returning to court if the person owing child support falls more than thirty days behind in payments. Wage withholding can be used to collect current support as well as past-due support.

Wage deduction orders are effective in collecting support if the parent is regularly employed and does not change jobs frequently. If the parent loses a job, there is of course no wage from which to make a deduction. If the parent changes jobs, the new employer must be served with a deduction notice before wages are withheld.

If a parent is self-employed, the parent is still obliged to send payments, but the person to whom support is due cannot look to an independent employer to make sure that payments are sent on time.

For parents who are behind in support payments, the state also can intercept federal and state tax refunds. This is a useful remedy if the obligor-parent has a sizeable refund due. If the obligor filed a joint income tax return with a new spouse, the new spouse can show the enforcement authorities the portion of the income tax refund that belongs to him or her so that the spouse's portion of the refund will not be intercepted. As a matter of pragmatics, the tax intercept usually is helpful for only one year. Once an obligor-parent has had a substantial tax refund seized, that parent often adjusts deductions of taxes from wages so that refunds in future years will be minimal.

In addition to seizing tax refunds, states also can place liens on property, such as real estate and automobiles, to obtain past-due support.

Another penalty that states may impose on parents who have not paid support is a finding of **contempt of court**. A finding of contempt of court means that the person charged with contempt has willfully not done something that he or she has been ordered to do by the court—in this case, to pay child support. A finding of contempt of court can result in a fine, a jail term, or both. If the parent cannot pay support for a good reason, such as loss of a job without fault of the parent, a court will not find the parent in contempt, but the obligation to pay support continues.

To enforce child support orders when the child lives in one state and the obligor lives in another state, several laws can be used to establish support orders and collect payments. The main two laws are the **Uniform Interstate Family Support Act (UIFSA)** and the **Uniform Reciprocal Enforcement of Support Act (URESA)**. These laws establish rules regarding which court or courts can set support and the procedures for collecting support between states.

State attorneys or district attorneys are available to help with collection of child support, though their efficiency varies from district to district. Some parents to whom support is due have complained of delays in handling of support claims. State attorneys provide their services at no costs to parents who are receiving public aid (Aid to Families with Dependent Children). For parents who do not receive public aid, the state attorney also can provide assistance, but a small charge (usually less than $100) may apply.

Private attorneys can help parents with collection of child support. The attorney's normal rates will apply, although some attorneys may be willing to handle the case for a **contingency fee**, which means the lawyer will take a portion of whatever is collected, but the client will not have to pay the attorney if nothing is collected. The permissibility of contingency fees to collect past-due support varies from state to state. The amount of the contingency fee also varies, but a payment to the attorney of one third of the amount collected is a common arrangement.

Attorney fees also can be assessed against the party who was supposed to pay support but did not. In that case, the parent who was supposed to pay support will pay for the attorney of the other parent in addition to his or her own attorney fees.

Another way of collecting past-due child support is to use a collection agency. Some collection agencies will handle collection of child support just as they handle collection of business debts or credit card debts. Collection agencies usually charge a contingency fee. Collection agencies can be found through the Yellow Pages (particularly the "Business" volume of the Yellow Pages, if there is a separate volume for business-related services).

Although prosecutors involved in punishing parents who do not

COLLECTING PAST-DUE CHILD SUPPORT

The following is a checklist of techniques for collection of past-due child support:

- **Wage withholding orders.** These are entered by a court and served on the employer of the parent who owes support. (The person who owes support is called the "obligor.") The employer sends payments to the government, which then sends support payments to the parent to whom support is owed.
- **Tax refund intercepts.** The government sends a notice to the Internal Revenue Service or the state department of revenue, directing that the obligor's tax refund be sent to the government for payment of support.
- **Liens on property.** A lien can be placed on the real estate, automobile, or other property of the obligor. If support is not paid, the property can be confiscated and sold. Alternatively, the lien may stay on the property until it is sold by the obligor, at which point the debt must be paid before the obligor receives any proceeds from the sale.
- **Contempt of court.** The person to whom support is due or the government can ask a court to hold the obligor in contempt of court for willful failure to pay support. If found guilty of contempt of court, the obligor can be jailed, fined, or both.
- **Collection agencies.** Some collection agencies are willing to help collect past-due support, just as they collect past-due commercial debts. Collection agencies usually charge a portion of the amount collected.
- **Revocation of licenses.** About twenty states will revoke the driver's license or professional licenses of persons who have not paid child support.
- **Interstate collections.** In addition to the remedies just listed, state and federal statutes are available to facilitate enforcement of support orders when the obligor and the person to whom support is due live in different states. State and federal prosecutors can help with interstate collections.

pay child support usually work for state or county governments, federal prosecutors can get involved too. In 1992 Congress passed the **Child Support Recovery Act,** which makes it a federal crime to willfully fail to pay child support to a child who resides in another state if the past-due amount has been unpaid for over one year or exceeds $5,000. Punishments under the federal law include up to six months' imprisonment and a $5,000 fine for a first offense, and up to two years' imprisonment and a $250,000 fine for a repeat offense.

Federal prosecutors have not actively used the new law to go after parents who do not pay child support. Most U.S. attorneys prefer to use their resources for larger-scale criminal activity. Attorney General Janet Reno has said that without more resources, federal prosecutors will focus on the most egregious cases and leave enforcement of other cases to the states.

For parents seeking government help in collecting child support, local prosecutors are likely to have more to offer than federal prosecutors, unless the amount of past-due support is very large and the obligor lives in a different state than the parent to whom support is due.

One egregious case that arose before passage of the federal law was handled by Arizona prosecutors. A thirty-five-year-old man was ordered to pay $600 per month support for his three children, but never paid a penny, according to Arizona child support officials. The man moved from state to state, changing the spelling of his name and his Social Security number four times in an effort to avoid collection of support. When prosecutors finally caught up with the man ten years after the original support order, the man owed $108,000 in past-due support and interest. He was sentenced to one and a half years in prison.

Most parents who owe support do not make such a career out of avoiding support obligations. Nonetheless, enforcement of support can be difficult.

As noted earlier, one of the most commonly used tools for collecting support—automatic deduction for the obligor's wages— works only if the parent to whom support is due or the government knows where the obligor is working *and* the obligor's employer has been served with papers ordering the employer to deduct child support payments from wages. Serving an employer with a deduction order is a simple process; it generally can be done by mail. But first, the government or parent to whom support is owed needs to know where the employer is.

To improve enforcement, some legislative leaders would like to enact a law that would direct the Internal Revenue Service (IRS) to supervise collection of child support. As of early 1996, such a law has not been passed.

Another technique to try to force payment of child support is to make the granting or renewal of certain types of licenses contingent on payment of support. If an obligor does not pay support, the obligor could lose his or her driver's license or professional license (such as a license to practice law or medicine or work as a barber, beautician, or plumber). Approximately twenty states have enacted such laws.

Maine was one of the first states to enact legislation to make licensing contingent upon payment of child support. Maine reported that as of early 1996, it had collected approximately $40 million in past-due support in the first two and a half years of the program. Maine found that the threat of license revocation often was enough to induce prompt payment. Of 21,000 persons who received warning letters from the state, well more than half of those persons made payments or entered into written agreements to make payments. After the warning letters were sent out, only 400 parents received formal notice that their licenses would be revoked in twenty-one days and, of those, forty-one actually lost their licenses.

Proponents of making licensing contingent upon payment of child support like the comparative simplicity of the approach. Revocation (or threats of revocation) of licenses can be handled administratively. In some states, such as Maine, court hearings are not necessary, as they are with some other remedies, such as actions for contempt of court.

Opponents of programs such as Maine's are concerned that an administrative system may not adequately take into account the hardship to an obligor who has lost a job or income and cannot afford to pay. If an obligor's professional license is revoked, the obligor's ability to pay may be harmed further.

Congress is considering passing a law that would require all states to make the granting of licenses contingent on paying child support.

CHILD SUPPORT AND VISITATION

Child support and visitation are independent rights and obligations. If a parent is not receiving child support, the remedy for that parent is to go to court (or activate a wage withholding order) to collect child support. The parent who is supposed to receive child support may not deny the noncustodial parent visitation or contact with the child because support was not paid.

Similarly, if visitation or contact with the child is blocked by the custodial parent, the legal remedy for the noncustodial parent is to go to court to obtain an order enforcing visitation. The noncustodial parent may not cut off or reduce child support because the custodial parent interfered with visitation.

■

CHAPTER TWELVE

Custody and Visitation

CHILD CUSTODY IS THE RIGHT AND DUTY to care for a child on a day-to-day basis and to make major decisions about the child.

In **sole custody** arrangements, one parent takes care of the child most of the time and makes major decisions about the child. That parent usually is called the **custodial parent**. The other parent generally is referred to as the **noncustodial parent**. The noncustodial parent almost always has a right of **visitation**—a right to be with the child, including for overnight visits and vacation periods.

In **joint custody** arrangements, both parents share in making major decisions, and both parents also might spend substantial amounts of time with the child.

As with financial issues in a divorce, most husbands and wives have reached an agreement on custody before they go to court. Fewer than 5 percent of parents have custody of their child decided by a judge.

When parents cannot agree on custody of their child, the court decides custody according to **the best interest of the child**. Determining the best interest of the child involves consideration of many factors. Those factors, along with more information about visitation and joint custody, will be discussed in later sections of this chapter.

EVOLUTION OF CUSTODY STANDARDS

The law of child custody has swung like a pendulum. From the early history of our country until the mid-1800s, fathers were favored for custody in the event of a divorce. Children were viewed as similar to property. If a husband and wife divorced, the man usually received the property—such as the farm or the family business. He also received custody of the children. Some courts viewed custody to the father as a natural extension of the father's duty to support and educate his children.

By the mid-1800s, most states switched to a strong preference for the mother. This preference often was referred to as the **Tender Years Doctrine** or **Maternal Presumption**. Under the Tender Years Doctrine, the mother received custody as long as she was minimally fit. In other words, in a contested custody case, a mother would receive custody unless there was something very wrong with her, such as mental illness, alcoholism, or an abusive relationship with her child. The parenting skills of the father were not relevant.

The automatic preference for mothers continued until the 1960s or 1980s, depending on the state. Then principles of equality took over, at least in the law books.

PREFERENCES FOR MOTHERS OR FATHERS

Under the current law of almost all states, mothers and fathers have an equal right to custody. Courts are not supposed to assume that a child is automatically better off with the mother or the father. In a contested custody case, both the father and mother have an equal burden of proving to the court that it is in the best interest of the child that the child be in his or her custody.

There are a few states (mostly in the South) that have laws providing that if everything else is equal, the mother may be preferred; but in those states, many fathers have been successful in obtaining custody, even if the mother is a fit parent.

In some states, courts say that mothers and fathers are to be considered equally, but the courts then go on to hold that it is permissible to consider the age or sex of the child when deciding custody. That usually translates to a preference for mothers if the child is young or female. But, again, it is possible for fathers in those states to gain custody, even when the mother is fit.

Although judges are supposed to be neutral in custody disputes between mothers and fathers, some judges appear to be biased. An advantage of having an attorney experienced in family law cases is that the attorney may know which judges may be biased and which may not. The attorney may know what types of evidence will appeal to the judge and which types will not.

In many jurisdictions, it is possible to obtain a change of judge by asking for it. Such a change often is called a **change of venue**. Generally, a litigant is entitled to one change of venue without having to present a reason. The request, however, must be made before the judge has ruled on substantive issues in the case. If one is faced with a judge one suspects of bias, a change of venue can be useful (although a litigant would want to consider the other judges to whom the case might be transferred and be reasonably sure that the change will not make the situation worse).

If a case is transferred to a judge who the litigant or the attorney does not like, it will be difficult to obtain a second change of venue. Courts to not wish to allow parties to keep bouncing cases between judges. Courts usually are unwilling to order a second change of venue unless there is a clear, specific showing of prejudice by the judge to whom the case has been transferred. If a parent is before a judge who is believed to be biased (and a change of venue cannot be obtained), the parent just puts on the strongest case possible and hopes for the best.

As a group, judges are less biased in deciding custody cases today than in times past, although most observers believe bias still exists.

Possible prejudice in favor of mothers. Judges, based on their background or personal experience, may have a deep-seated belief that mothers can take care of children better than fathers and that fathers have little experience in parenting. Such judges may bring those views to the bench, in which case a father may have a very difficult time gaining custody.

A Louisiana case illustrates the point. The trial judge gave custody to the mother saying, "It is just a physiological fact that girl children should be with their mother if there are no serious differences." Since the trial judge's bias was clear on the record, the appellate court reversed the decision and ordered that there be further proceedings—without applying improper presumptions based on sex of the parents.

In cases in which the trial judge is less explicit about his or her prejudice, it may be more difficult to obtain a reversal if the trial judge was prejudiced.

Possible prejudice in favor of fathers. As noted in the section on evolution of custody standards, prejudice based on sex of the parent is not a one-way street. Sometimes prejudice runs in favor of fathers.

Some judges tend to automatically favor fathers, particularly if the children are boys. In an Iowa case, for example, a trial judge gave custody of two boys, ages nine and eleven, to the father, saying that the father "will be able to engage in various activities with boys, such as athletic events, fishing, hunting, mechanical training, and other activities boys are interested in."

The trouble was that the testimony before the court did not support the judge's presumption. The record in the case did not show that the boys were interested in hunting or mechanical training or that the father's skills in those areas were superior to the mother's. In fact, the mother went fishing with the boys more often than the father did.

The Iowa Supreme Court reversed and gave custody to the mother, who had been primarily responsible for raising the children. The court said, "The real issue is not the sex of the parent but which parent will do better in raising the children. It logically follows that neither parent has an edge based on the sex of the children either."

Another possible prejudice in favor of fathers may be regarded as a prejudice against working mothers. In some cases, it appears that judges have looked askance at working mothers, perhaps holding mothers to a higher standard than fathers and viewing a working mother as not serving the best interest of her child. Such judges also may view a father who shows slightly above-average involvement in parenting as "exceptional" and reward him with custody.

It is difficult to assess how widespread this view may be among judges. Some commentators assert that bias against working mothers, especially professional women, may be a significant factor. Others suggest that a review of appellate court cases does not disclose widespread prejudice against working mothers, although it exists to some degree. If anything, most judges seem to admire a mother (or father) who can simultaneously manage work and raising children.

A parent's work schedule normally is not a decisive factor in custody, unless there is a major difference in the amount of time each parent can spend with the child. If after a divorce, one parent will be able to spend much more time with the child than the other parent, that is a factor in favor of the parent with the more flexible schedule.

CUSTODY FACTORS

PRIMARY CARETAKER OF THE CHILD

There is no one factor that is invariably "the" most important factor in a custody case. The importance of a particular factor will vary with the facts of each case. If one parent in a custody dispute has a major problem with alcoholism or mental illness or has abused the child, that of course could be the deciding factor.

If neither parent has engaged in unusually bad conduct, the most important factor often is which parent has been primarily responsible for taking care of the child on a day-to-day basis. Some states refer to this as **the primary caretaker factor**. If one parent can show that he or she took care of the child most of the time, that parent usually will be favored for custody, particularly if the child is young (under approximately eight years old).

Use of this factor promotes continuity in the child's life and gives custody of the child to the more experienced parent who has taken care of the child's day-to-day needs. If both parents have actively cared for the child or if the child is older, the factor is less crucial, although it is still considered.

One state (West Virginia) has taken use of the primary caretaker factor a step further. In West Virginia, a primary caretaker is automatically entitled to custody as long as he or she is minimally fit. The presumption does not apply if the child is old enough to express an intelligent preference for a parent other than the primary caretaker. In other states, determination of which parent is the primary caretaker is an important factor, but it is not the sole deciding factor.

CHILD'S PREFERENCES

The wishes of a child can be an important factor in deciding custody. The weight a court gives the child's wishes will depend on the child's age, maturity, and quality of reasons. Some judges do not even listen to the preferences of a child under the age of seven and instead assume the child is too young to express an informed preference.

A court is more likely to follow the preferences of an older child, although the court will want to assess the quality of the child's reasons. If a child wants to be with the parent who offers more freedom and less discipline, a judge is not likely to honor the preference. A child whose reasons are vague or whose answers seem coached also may not have his or her preferences followed.

On the other hand, if a child expresses a good reason related to the child's best interest—such as genuinely feeling closer to one parent than the other—the court probably will follow the preference. Although most states treat a child's wishes as only one factor to be considered, two states (Georgia and West Virginia) declare that a child of fourteen has an "absolute right" to choose the parent with whom the child will live, as long as the parent is fit.

If a judge decides to talk with the child, the judge usually will do so in private, in the judge's chambers rather than in open court. Generally, the parents are not in the room when the judge talks to the child, although the parents' attorneys might be. In some cases, the judge may appoint a mental health professional, such as a psychiatrist, psychologist, or social worker, to talk to the child and report to the court.

NONMARITAL SEXUAL RELATIONSHIPS

The impact of a parent's nonmarital sexual relationships on a custody determination depends on the law of the state and the facts of the case. In most states, affairs or nonmarital sexual relations are not supposed to be a factor in deciding custody unless it can be shown that the relationship has harmed the child or is likely to harm the child in the future.

If, for example, one parent has had a discreet affair during the marriage, that normally would not be a significant factor in deciding custody. Similarly, if after the marriage is over, a parent lives with a person to whom he or she is not married, the live-in relationship by itself normally is not a major factor in deciding custody. In the case of live-in relationships, the quality of the relationship between the child and the live-in partner can be an important factor in a custody dispute.

If the parent's nonmarital sexual relationship or relationships have placed the child in embarrassing situations or caused significant stress to the child, then the relationship would be a negative factor against the parent involved in the relationship. In one case, for example, a mother conducted an affair during her marriage with a man who lived in the neighborhood. She and the neighbor periodically were involved in the woman's bedroom while the husband was out and the child was home.

This placed the child in a stressful situation—a situation that grew worse when the wife of the neighbor appeared at the door and demanded that the child tell her what the child's mother and neighbor were doing in the bedroom. The mother lost custody primarily because of her nonmarital relationship and its impact on the child.

Although most states require a specific showing of harm to the child before nonmarital sexual conduct is considered, courts in a few states are more inclined to automatically assume that a parent's nonmarital sexual relationship is harmful to the child or will be harmful to the child. As with the issue of a preference for mothers or fathers in custody cases, the issue of a parent's sexual conduct can be one in which individual judges may allow personal biases to influence their decisions.

HOMOSEXUAL RELATIONSHIPS

The impact of a parent's homosexual relationships on custody decisions varies dramatically from state to state. Courts in many states are more willing to assume harmful impact to a child from a parent's homosexual relationship than from a heterosexual relationship. On the other hand, some states treat homosexual and heterosexual relationships equally and will not consider the relationship to be a significant factor unless specific harm to the child is shown.

A homosexual parent (or a heterosexual parent) seeking custody will have a stronger case if he or she presents evidence that the child does not witness sexual contact between the partners and that the child likes the parent's partner.

UNDERMINING CHILD'S RELATIONSHIP WITH OTHER PARENT

Most states declare a specific policy favoring an ongoing, healthy relationship between the child and both parents. If one parent is trying to undermine the child's relationship with the other parent, that is a negative factor against the parent who is trying to hurt the relationship. If other factors are close to equal, a court may grant custody to the parent who is more likely to encourage an open and good relationship with the other parent.

Similarly, if a custodial parent regularly interferes with visitation, that is a negative factor against the custodial parent and can lead to modification of custody to the noncustodial parent (assuming the noncustodial parent is able to properly care for the child).

RELIGIOUS BELIEFS AND PRACTICES

Under the First Amendment to the United States Constitution, both parents have a right to practice religion or not practice religion as they see fit. A judge is not supposed to make value judgments about whether a child is better off with or without religious training or about which religion is better. If a child has been brought up with particular religious beliefs and religious activities are important to the child, a court might favor promoting continuity in the child's life, but the court should not favor religion *per se*.

In some cases, a parent's unusual or nonmainstream religious activities may become an issue. Normally, a court should not consider a parent's unusual religious practices in deciding custody or visitation unless specific harm to the child is shown. If, because of a parent's religious beliefs, a parent has not given the child needed medical care or has tried to convince the child that the other parent is evil and should not be associated with, that could be a basis for placing custody with the parent whose religious conduct does not harm the child.

MODIFICATION OF CUSTODY

Courts have the power to modify child custody arrangements to meet the needs of the child and to respond to changes in the parents' lives.

A parent seeking to change custody through the court usually must show that the conditions have changed substantially since the last custody order. The change of circumstance usually involves something negative in the child's current environment—such as improper supervision, or harmful conflicts with the custodial parent or stepparent.

A child's preference to live with the noncustodial parent can be a basis for modifying custody, but the child's reasons must be well based and not appear to be the result of coaching or bribery. In one case, a father was trying to gain custody of his thirteen-year-old son. In the days before the custody hearing, the father presented his son with a series of gifts reminiscent of the song "The Twelve Days of Christmas." Among the acquisitions of the boy: a horse, two television sets, a minibike, a shotgun, a motorcycle, and a private telephone. The father did not gain custody.

In addition to showing a change in circumstances, the parent seeking a change of custody must show that he or she can provide a better environment for the child than the child's current environment. But in order to discourage parents from constantly litigating custody, some states apply a special standard for custody modifications sought within the first year or two after a prior custody order. In those states, the parent must show not only a change of circumstances, but also that the child is endangered by the child's current environment. After expiration of the one- or two-year period, the courts apply normal standards for modification (without having to show endangerment).

If parents voluntarily wish to change custody or the visitation schedule (see below), they may do so without having to prove special factors such as endangerment or a change in circumstances. Parents may change custody and visitation without obtaining a court order, but if the parent receiving custody or more visitation wants to make the modification "official"—thus making it more difficult for the other parent to go back to the old system—it is best to obtain a court order modifying custody and visitation.

In addition, an informal change of custody will not necessarily stop a parent's support obligation—only a court order can provide certainty of that.

VERY SPECIFIC CUSTODY AND VISITATION ORDERS

If parents are prone to conflict or if they like a high level of detail, it may be desirable to have a very specific custody and visitation order covering a multitude of issues, including:

- Specification of weekends of visitation (perhaps with reference to weekends that begin on the first, third, and fifth Fridays of the month)
- Lists of holidays, winter breaks, and spring breaks, perhaps using odd and even years to keep track of which parent has which holidays in a given year
- Allocation of special school holidays and institute days (that may not be the same as legal holidays)
- Specific pick-up and drop-off times
- Designation of which parent will hold the birthday parties to which the child invites friends—perhaps alternating years
- Periods of notice required for choosing summer vacation time with the children
- Notification of where the child will be when out of town

VISITATION

A parent who does not receive custody normally is entitled to visitation with the child. The amount of visitation will vary with the desires of the parents and the inclinations of the judge. A common amount of visitation, however, is: every other weekend (Friday evening through Sunday); a weeknight (for dinner); half of the child's winter and spring breaks, alternate major holidays; and two to six weeks in the summer.

If parents live far apart and regular weekend visitation is not feasible, it is common to allocate more summer vacation and school holidays to the noncustodial parent.

For parents who do not like the terms "visitation" or "custody,"

- Agreements for parents to try to accommodate each other if the parents must travel out of town on business or are otherwise not able to be with the child for a designated period
- Agreements to share or provide copies of school and medical records (federal law requires that both parents have access to school records unless a court orders otherwise)
- Agreements to notify the other parent of teacher conferences, athletic events, and other events involving the child
- Agreements for the parents to consult with each other about what extracurricular activities the child will be involved in
- Agreements to make the child available for special events regardless of the custody or visitation schedule—for example, to make the child available for family weddings, reunions, and funerals
- Agreements to allow the child telephone contact with the other parent (times and frequency could be specified)
- Agreements to not interfere with (or to perhaps encourage) the child's relationship with the other parent
- Agreements to notify the other parent of change in address, telephone number, or employment

it is possible to draft a custody and visitation order that leaves out those terms and just describes the times at which the child will be with each parent.

A court can deny or restrict visitation if the court believes the child might be placed in danger by visitation. For example, if the noncustodial parent has molested the child, is likely to kidnap the child, or is likely to use illegal drugs or excessive amounts of alcohol while caring for the child, a court probably will deny visitation or restrict visitation. If visitation is restricted, visitation might be allowed only under supervision, such as at a social service agency or in the company of a responsible relative.

For discussion of visitation rights of grandparents and stepparents, see pages 142 to 143.

JOINT CUSTODY

Joint custody—sometimes referred to as **shared custody** or **shared parenting**—has two parts: joint legal custody and joint physical custody. A joint custody order can have one or both parts.

Joint legal custody refers to both parents sharing in major decisions affecting the child. The custody order may describe the issues on which the parents must share decisions. The most common issues are school, health care, and religious training (although both parents have a right to expose the child to their respective religious beliefs). Other issues on which the parents may make joint decisions include: extracurricular activities, summer camp, age for dating or driving, and methods of discipline.

Many joint custody orders specify procedures parents should follow in the event they cannot agree on an issue. The most common procedure is for the parents to consult a mediator. (Mediation is discussed in chapter 15.)

Joint physical custody refers to the time the child spends with each parent. The amount of time is flexible. The length of time could be relatively moderate, such as every other weekend with one parent; or the amount of time could be equally divided between the parents. Parents who opt for equal time sharing have come up with many alternatives such as: alternate two-day periods; equal division of the week; alternate weeks; alternate months; and alternate six-month periods.

If the child is attending school and spends a substantial amount of time with both parents, it usually is best for the child if the parents live relatively close to each other. Some parents, on an interim basis, have kept the child in a single home and the parents rotate staying in the home with the child.

In most states, joint custody is an option, just as sole custody is an option. Courts may order joint custody or sole custody according to what the judge thinks is in the best interest of the child. In some states (eleven in 1995), legislatures have declared a preference for joint custody. That usually means the courts are supposed to order joint custody if a parent asks for it, unless there is a good reason for not ordering joint custody.

The most common reason for not ordering joint custody is the parents' inability to cooperate. Courts are concerned that a child will be caught in the middle of a tug-of-war if joint custody is ordered for parents who do not cooperate with each other. Parents who do not cooperate also will have trouble with sole custody and visitation, but the frequency of conflicts may be somewhat less, since they will need to confer less often on major decisions and the logistics of a joint physical custody arrangement.

Supporters of joint physical custody stress that it is in the best interest of the child to protect and promote the child's relationship with both parents. They believe shared custody is the best way to make sure that the child does not "lose" a parent because of the divorce. Supporters of joint custody also argue that it is the natural right of parents to be joint custodians of their children, whether the parents are married or not.

Critics of joint custody fear that joint custody is unworkable and worry about instability and potential conflict for the child. The success of joint physical custody may depend on the child. Some researchers have said that children who are relatively relaxed and laid back will do better with joint physical custody than children who are tense and become easily upset by changes in routine. Because joint physical custody usually requires keeping two homes for the child, joint physical custody often costs more than sole custody.

Children's needs for each parent change as they grow. Parents probably should avoid locking in any parenting plan forever. Rather, they should plan to review the custody and visitation arrangement as the children grow and the children's needs change.

OUT-OF-STATE MOVES WITH THE CHILD

The right of a parent to move out of state with the child is another area of law on which states are divided. In times past, most states automatically would allow the custodial parent to move wherever he or she wanted with the child.

In recent years, many states have placed restrictions on the right of the custodial parent to move with the child. These states have a strong policy in favor of preserving continuity in the relationship between the child and noncustodial parent, and courts in these states are reluctant to allow the custodial parent to move with the child over the objection of the noncustodial parent unless there is a very good reason for the move.

In these states, the law may say a child cannot be moved without permission of the other parent or permission of the court. A parent who seeks to move with the child may be required to give reasonable notice (such as sixty days) before a proposed moving date.

The law in this area is shifting. Many state legislatures are considering new standards for determining when a parent can move out of state with the child. Regardless of the law in a particular state, there are several factors that courts consider when deciding whether to allow a move with the child:

- **Custodial parent's reason for the move.** If the parent who seeks to move with the child has a good faith reason for the move, that is a positive factor in favor of the move. Good faith reasons include: obtaining a better job, joining a new spouse, and moving to be near extended family. If a job change is the basis for the move, the plan for a new job should be specific, not just a general hope of finding new employment.

The main bad faith reason for moving is to deprive the noncustodial parent of contact with the child. If the court believes the main reason for the move is to diminish contact between the child and the noncustodial parent, the court is not likely to allow the move.

- **Noncustodial parent's reason for opposing the move.** If the noncustodial parent has a good reason for opposing the move, that is a factor in favor of denying permission for the move. The main good reason for opposing relocation is the child's close relationship with the noncustodial parent and the disruption of frequent contact between the child and noncustodial parent that would result from the move. If the noncustodial parent is not close to the child or has not regularly exercised visitation, the court is more likely to allow the move.

- **Advantages to the child from the move.** If it can be shown the child will benefit from the move, that of course is a factor in favor of the move. If, for example, the child will go to a better school or be in a climate that is better for the child's health, those factors will support the request for the move. The parent asserting that the child will benefit from relocation should be ready with specific evidence, such as witnesses knowledgeable about the difference in school systems or medical testimony regarding the child's health.

- **The degree to which visitation can be restructured to preserve the relationship between the child and the noncustodial parent.** If the court believes that reasonable restructuring of visitation can preserve and promote a good relationship between the child and the noncustodial parent, that is a factor in favor of allowing the move. Restructuring of visitation usually involves scheduling more visitation in the summer and over other holiday breaks. In some cases, the noncustodial parent and child may actually spend more time together each year under the restructured schedule than under the original schedule, although visitation will be less frequent under the restructured schedule. If the court believes that frequency of contact is more important than large blocks of time, then the move is less likely. If the parents cannot afford visits over a long distance, the court also is less likely to allow relocation. If visitation is affordable, the court might reduce child support to facilitate visits, or the court might assess the cost of travel on the parent who seeks to move.

If the parents have joint physical custody, with both parents spending a substantial amount of time with the child, a court may treat the request to move like an original custody determination. The court will try to decide which parent will best meet the child's needs. The court will consider the above factors, along with other factors usually considered in custody cases, including the child's attachment to the current home, school, and community.

RIGHTS OF GRANDPARENTS

The statutes of all states give grandparents a right to visit with their grandchildren. The scope of that right varies from state to state. In most states, if the parents of a child are divorced or separated, the grandparents may seek a specific order of visitation.

Generally, an order of visitation for the grandparents will not be necessary if the grandparents will be able to see their grandchildren at times when the grandchildren are with their parent to whom the grandparent is related. If, however, such contact is not feasible because the parent does not regularly exercise visitation, then specific visitation for the grandparents may be ordered.

Most states also allow grandparent visitation if the parent to whom the grandparent is related has died. Some states also will give grandparents visitation if the child had lived with the grandparents for a significant period of time, such as one year.

If the grandparent seeks visitation with the child, the grandparent must show that visitation is in the best interest if the child. Best interest of the child usually is found if the grandparents have had a good relationship with the grandchild in the past and if the grandparents will not use their visitation to undermine the child's relationship with the parent or parents.

A few courts and legislatures have extended the right to grandparent visitation in cases in which the parents are not divorced and are still living together. Two state supreme courts, however, have held that such visitation is an unconstitutional intrusion into the parents' family privacy.

It is possible for grandparents to obtain custody of grandchildren.

If the parents consent to custody by the grandparents, the grandparents may have custody on an informal basis. Alternatively, grandparents may seek to formalize the arrangement by going to court to be named guardians of their grandchild. Some school districts may require that a grandparent be named guardian of the child before the grandparent may enroll the grandchild in school.

If grandparents seek custody of the grandchild over the parents' objection, the grandparents usually will have to show that the parents are unfit—a heavy burden of proof.

If, however, the grandparents have been raising their grandchild for a considerable length of time under an informal arrangement, the grandparents may have become the "psychological parents" of the grandchild by the time the parent or parents seek to regain custody. In this circumstance, courts in many states will allow the grandparents to retain custody, even if the parents are fit.

RIGHTS AND DUTIES OF STEPPARENTS

The responsibilities of a stepparent depend on state law. A stepparent usually is not required to pay child support for a spouse's child from another marriage, unless the stepparent has adopted the child. Until then, the child's biological parents are liable for the child's support. Some states, however, make stepparents liable for the stepchild's support as long as the stepparent and stepchild are living together.

A stepparent who does not adopt a spouse's child normally may not claim custody of the child if the marriage ends in divorce, although some states allow a stepparent to seek visitation.

A stepchild usually does not share in the estate of a stepparent, unless the stepparent has provided for the stepchild in a will. However, an unmarried stepchild under eighteen may receive supplemental retirement benefits or survivor's benefits under Social Security.

CHAPTER THIRTEEN

■

Domestic Violence

IN THE UNITED STATES, there were an average of 621,015 acts of domestic violence per year reported to law enforcement agencies between 1987 and 1991, according to the United States Justice Department Bureau of Justice Statistics. (Those are the most recent figures available as of 1996.) The acts of violence included assaults, rapes, and robberies.

According to the Justice Department, 92 percent of victims of domestic violence were female; only 8 percent of victims were male. The most frequent attackers were boyfriends or girlfriends—51 percent of all attackers. Thirty-four percent of attackers were spouses, and 15 percent were former spouses.

Although most studies show that women are the primary victims of domestic violence, some studies suggest that about half of domestic violence cases are **bi-directional**—meaning both the man and woman are engaging in aggressive conduct. Abused women are more likely to report domestic violence to the police than abused men.

The rate of domestic violence against white women and black women was about the same (5 per 1,000 per year). The rate also was similar between Hispanic and non-Hispanic females (6 per 1,000).

Incidence of domestic violence correlated with income. Women with family income under $9,999 experienced the highest rates of violence (11 per 1,000); women with family income over $30,000 had the lowest rates of violence (2 per 1,000).

Of the 22,540 murders committed in the United States in 1992, approximately 15 percent were committed by "intimates" (spouse, ex-spouse, boyfriend, or girlfriend of the victim). Over half the persons accused of murdering their spouse had been drinking alcohol at the time of the murder.

The Justice Department survey found that 80 percent of women took self-protective action in response to domestic violence. Forty percent of the responses were described as "physical action," and another 40 percent were described as "passive/verbal." Of the women who tried to protect themselves against domestic violence, over half believed their self-protective response helped the situation and almost one quarter believed their action made the situation worse.

STATE LAWS

In recent years, state legislatures and courts have been paying increasing attention to domestic violence. Many states have elaborate laws designed to protect individuals from domestic violence by their spouses, other family members, and people with whom the victim may have had a social relationship.

A common remedy is for a court to issue an **order of protection** (also known as a **protective order**) that orders the alleged abuser to stop abusing or harassing someone else. In addition, the orders often will direct the abuser to stay away from the spouse, the spouse's home, or place of work. If the person continues to abuse his or her spouse (or another person protected by the order), the abuser can be charged with a criminal violation of the order in addition to being charged with other offenses, such as assault and battery. Penalties include fines and incarceration.

The domestic violence statutes in most states apply not only to physical attacks, but also to other types of conduct. Some examples of conduct that could be considered domestic violence: creating disturbance at a spouse's place of work, placing harassing telephone calls, stalking, using surveillance, and making threats against a spouse or family member (even though the threat may not have been carried out).

Studies have shown that issuing a protective order or arresting a person who commits an act of domestic violence does reduce future incidents of domestic violence. When perpetrators of domestic violence see that the police and court system will treat domestic violence seriously, many persons who commit domestic violence may be deterred from future violence.

But orders of protection are not guarantees of protection or safety. For some individuals with intense anger or rage, no court order will stop their violence, and a court order might even add to the rage. Newspapers periodically carry stories of women murdered by their husband or boyfriend despite numerous arrests and orders of protection. The legal system cannot offer perfect protection, although it can reduce violence.

FEDERAL LAW

In 1994 Congress enacted the **Violence Against Women Act.** The more formal title of the new law is the **Civil Rights Remedies for Gender-Motivated Violence Act.** Prior to this statute, laws against domestic violence were almost exclusively at the state level.

The Violence Against Women Act allows a person to sue for damages if another person "commits a crime of violence motivated by gender." The new law is part of the federal government's civil rights statute. If the crime of violence constitutes a felony against the person or the property of the victim, the victim can sue the assailant for both **compensatory damages** and **punitive damages.**

Compensatory damages are designed to compensate the victim for the loss. The damages could include medical expenses, lost wages, pain, and suffering. Punitive damages are an added amount of damages—not for the purpose of compensation—but rather for the purpose of punishing the assailant and deterring future abusive conduct. Punitive damages, however, are still paid to the victim.

Under the federal law, a victim of domestic violence also can seek **injunctive relief** or **declaratory relief.** This is basically the same as the order of protection that was discussed in the last section on "State Laws Regarding Domestic Violence."

The Violence Against Women Act allows a successful party to collect attorney's fees in addition to damages. Legal actions under the act may be brought in state or federal courts.

As a matter of pragmatics, it probably would not be worth the victim's effort to sue under this new federal law unless the assailant has enough income and assets to pay damages. If the victim's main goal is to obtain an order prohibiting future abusive conduct, the laws of most states will do as well as the federal law.

WHERE TO TURN FOR HELP

In a crisis situation, a call to the police is a good place to start. Many people complain that police do not take accusations of domestic violence seriously. That can be true in some circumstances, but on the whole, police are treating domestic violence situations more seriously, and police officers are receiving increased training on the subject.

The local state attorney or district attorney also may be able to offer some help. An increasing number of hospitals, crisis intervention programs, domestic violence shelters, and social service agencies have programs to help victims of domestic violence. Agencies offering help in cases of domestic violence might be found in the Yellow Pages under "Domestic Violence Help," "Human Services Organizations," or "Crisis Intervention."

If one is working with an attorney in connection with a divorce, the attorney also should be able to initiate the appropriate legal proceedings. Additional resources are listed in the "Domestic Violence" entry in the appendix, "Where to Get More Information."

CHAPTER FOURTEEN

■

Working with an Attorney

An opening question when faced with a legal problem is: "Is it necessary to hire an attorney?"

The answer—as you probably can guess—is: "It depends."

There is not a single, easy-to-apply answer for all situations. The need for an attorney varies with the situation. Many factors should be considered. Among them:

- **How important is the issue?** For example, in a divorce, if there is a lot of money in dispute or if custody of children is genuinely at issue, an attorney's help probably is necessary. Conversely, if the dollar amount in dispute is low and no other important matters are at issue, an attorney's help may not be necessary.

- **How well do you understand the issue?** If you have been served with a pile of legal papers from someone who is suing you and you don't understand what the papers mean or what you should do next, you should consult an attorney. If you do understand the legal issues and the steps you need to take, your need for an attorney may be less.

- **How emotionally involved are you and how much negotiation is necessary?** The old adage goes, "A person who represents himself has a fool for a client." Much of the time (maybe most of the time) that is true, but some people are good at representing themselves. A key issue in deciding to represent oneself instead of hiring a lawyer is one's level of emotional involvement and ability to take a detached view of the controversy. If a person is very angry at the opposing party (such as in a bitterly contested divorce or contested adoption), it is best to have independent legal help to present the case in an organized, professional manner. If a person can keep a lid on his or her emotions and present logical arguments in negotiations, the person may be able to represent himself or herself effectively.

- **How user-friendly is the court system?** Some court systems are set up to help people handle their own legal disputes. The court may have forms with clear explanations to help people initiate legal actions or respond to a legal action. Clerks and judges might be willing to tell people, step-by-step, what they need to do and what their rights are. Other court systems are the opposite (or somewhere in between). Procedures may be complex and difficult for even lawyers to follow. Clerks and judges may seem to go out of their way to be nasty and make litigants feel like they are subhuman for taking up thirty seconds of the clerk's or judge's time. To get a sense of the degree to which the court system accommodates people who represent themselves, a visit to the courthouse or a call to the clerk of court with some polite questions may give an answer. You also might ask friends about their experience with the local court if the friends have dealt with issues similar to yours.

- **How much does legal representation cost?** An important factor in deciding to represent oneself, of course, is the cost of legal representation. For some, the cost of full-scale legal representation may not seem affordable. When involved in any legal dispute, one needs to do a cost-benefit analysis and ask, "Is pursuit of this case (or some issue in the case) sufficiently important to be worth the cost in money, time, and emotional energy?" If the stakes are high, full-scale representation may be worth the money and even save dollars or something else of great value later on. If the stakes are small, legal representation may not be cost-effective. One needs to calibrate the level of representation to the importance of the issue and the resources available to pursue the matter. This may mean full-scale representation, limited-purpose representation, or no representation. (Limited-purpose representation will be discussed further at the end of this section.)

Here are some examples of specific situations in which a lawyer is or is not necessary in connection with a divorce:

A man and woman have been married for two years. They have no children. Both work and are capable of self-support. They decide the marriage is a mistake, and although they each have some anger at the other, they are able to agree on how to divide the property they have. Each keeps what he or she brought into the marriage, and they will divide approximately equally a joint money market account after they pay off their MasterCard debt. If their main goal is to end the marriage, and go their separate ways without financial support from the other, neither the man nor the woman may need a lawyer. If the court system is user-friendly, they may be able to process their own divorce. However, if the court system is complicated or if they do not want to be bothered with learning how to do the paperwork, one of them may hire a lawyer to process the divorce and the other can choose to be unrepresented and consent to the terms of the divorce.

Another example: A woman and man have been married for twenty years. They have three children, ages nine to sixteen. The husband owns his own business—a chain of snack shops. The wife stayed home to take care of the children for eight years; she has worked part-time since then. The husband wants a divorce. The wife does not, but she realizes the divorce is inevitable. They dispute many issues, including the value of the husband's business, the disposition of the home, the wife's request for alimony, and the amount of child support. In this case, both the wife and husband need representation. Expert advice probably will be necessary to determine the value of the business, division of property, and support for the wife and children. If the wife does not trust the husband's financial statements, that is all the more reason to obtain legal help. If one party is seeking a portion of a retirement or profit-sharing plan established by the other, a lawyer's services will be necessary to draw up the appropriate papers to divide the parties' interest in the plan and avoid adverse tax consequences.

A final example: Husband and wife, both thirty-five, dispute custody of their children, ages five and seven. Both want sole custody. Both have been actively involved in raising the children. The husband and wife will need representation if the issue of custody will be contested in court. The emotional issue of custody usually is too sensitive for a mother or father to put on their own trial. Before going to court, however, the parties may wish to see if they can settle their dispute through use of a mediator. A mediator usually is a mental health professional or a lawyer who will work with the parties to attempt to reach a solution acceptable to them and in the best interest of the children. The next chapter will discuss mediation and other alternative means of dispute resolution.

When seeking legal help, or when considering whether or not to represent yourself, keep in mind it is not always necessary to hire a lawyer for full-scale representation. One can hire a lawyer for a limited purpose. For example, at the beginning of a dispute (or in the middle of a dispute), a lawyer can be hired just to give advice or review a document. You can pay the lawyer for one to three hours of consultations—explaining the facts of the case to the lawyer and seeking the lawyer's advice about your rights, additional steps you will need to take, and the likely outcome of the case. You can then tailor your plans for handling the case based on the perspectives gained from the lawyer. The use of a lawyer for a limited purpose rather than full representation sometimes is referred to as **unbundling** of legal services.

Lawyers also can be hired for the purpose of negotiating a settlement without the client committing to hire the lawyer for a long, expensive trial. Even if a person already has a lawyer, he or she can consider hiring another lawyer—not for full representation, but for a second opinion. Just as patients often want a second opinion before undertaking major medical treatment, it can be prudent to seek a second legal opinion before taking a major legal action that could impact one's life for years to come.

FINDING A LAWYER

Just as there are specialists in medicine, there are specialists in law. Some lawyers practice exclusively or primarily in family law. The need for a specialist will vary with the case. If there are complex issues of property or custody, it probably is best to seek a lawyer with substantial experience in family law. If a person wants to adopt a child to whom the adopting parent is not related, it also is best to work with a lawyer who has significant experience in the area, particularly if the adoption involves a child from another country or if the adoption is arranged privately rather than through an agency.

If one is adopting a child that is already in the family and no one is contesting the adoption, the procedure is more routine and could probably be handled by a nonspecialist. For example, if an aunt and uncle were adopting a nephew following death of the parents, or if a stepfather were adopting his stepchild without opposition from the biological father, the adoption should be quick and simple. (It might even be done by the adoptive parents themselves without need of an attorney.)

Hiring a specialist in family law does not necessarily cost more than hiring an attorney in general practice, although if one is seeking an attorney with a very good reputation in any field, the fees are likely to be higher than for other attorneys.

Seventeen states certify attorneys as specialists in areas of practice. The requirements for specialist certification vary from state to state, but they usually require several years of experience in the area of speciality and demonstration of knowledge in the area, such as through an examination (beyond the basic bar examination necessary for lawyers in most states). Six states that certify specialists in family law or domestic relations are: Arizona, Florida, California, New Mexico, North Carolina, and Texas. In states without official certification of specialists, lawyers often specialize; they are just not officially recognized as such by a state licensing agency.

There is also a national organization that certifies family law specialists. It is called the **American Academy of Matrimonial Lawyers**. The academy is a private organization of about 1,500 members. In order to become a member of the academy, a lawyer needs to have devoted 75 percent or more of his or her practice to family law for a period of at least ten years. Written or oral examinations are required, along with recommendations from judges and other lawyers. Membership in the academy does not automatically guarantee that the lawyer is good, but it does mean the lawyer has substantial experience in family law.

A person looking for a referral to a member of the American Academy of Matrimonial Lawyers can contact the academy at 150 N. Michigan Avenue, suite 2040, Chicago, Illinois 60601; telephone (312) 263-6477. The academy also has chapters in many states.

Usually state, county, and city bar associations will also make referrals to lawyers. Bar associations vary in the degree to which they screen lawyers to whom they make referrals. Some bar associations will make referrals to lawyers who declare themselves available to practice in a particular field. Other bar associations may require lawyers to submit proof that the lawyer has experience in the area. When calling a bar association's general telephone number, ask for the association's lawyer referral service.

If the person looking for a lawyer is low on funds, a possible source of help is a law school's legal clinic. Legal clinics sometimes will take family law cases at no charge or a low charge to the client. Clinics are staffed by law students working under the supervision of professors and attorneys. If the law school clinic is not able to take the case, the clinic may be able to refer the client to other low-cost legal services.

Legal Assistance Foundations (LAFs) have been established in some areas. LAFs are not-for-profit organizations that offer free or discounted legal help in civil cases, including family law cases.

Another source of referrals to lawyers working in family law can be the Yellow Pages or newspaper ads. As with any advertising, the phrase "Let the buyer beware" applies. Quality of lawyering is not necessarily proportional to the size or stylishness of an advertisement. If the advertisement proudly proclaims that the lawyer handles not only divorces but also drunk driving cases, wills, personal injury claims, real estate, bankruptcy, and incorporation, the client most likely will be dealing with a lawyer who is a generalist rather than a specialist. The lawyer may also prefer high-volume, quickly handled cases to complicated, time-intensive cases. As noted before, that can be fine for some cases, but not for others.

Friends and colleagues (including lawyers who work in areas other than family law) may be able to recommend a lawyer. If the friend is basing the recommendation on personal experience, try to find out more about the friend's case and how similar the friend's case is to yours. What was at issue? Property? Support? Custody? How complicated was the case? How diligent and approachable was the lawyer?

Within family law, lawyers also may specialize or have areas in which they are particularly good (or not so good). Some lawyers are masterful at finding hidden assets and dealing with complex financial issues, but the same lawyer may not be as talented at handling the high emotions and more subjective issues of a custody case. Some lawyers are good at both. Lawyers who handle adoptions may not handle divorces, and vice versa.

When talking with a lawyer, try to get a sense of the lawyer's experience with and comfort in handling the issues in your case.

LAWYERS' FEES

The amount of a lawyer's fee varies with the level of experience and locale of the lawyer. The more experience, expertise, and skill a lawyer has, the higher the fee (usually, but not always). Lawyers in urban areas generally charge more than lawyers in rural areas. The rates of suburban lawyers often are in between.

Most family lawyers charge on an hourly basis. Their fees will be equal to the total of the hours spent on the case times the lawyer's hourly rate. Different lawyers within a firm may have different hourly rates. Some lawyers charge different rates for appearing in court and for working in their offices. (The courtroom rate is higher on the theory that working in court involves extra skills and pressure. Other lawyers view their office skills and courtroom skills as equally valuable and thus charge the same rate for both types of service.)

A lawyer's time that is billed to a client is not just the time the lawyer spends with the client or in court. Lawyers may spend a significant amount of time in their offices reviewing documents, conducting research, planning strategy, talking to witnesses, talking to the opposing counsel, drafting letters, and preparing papers for filing in court.

If other lawyers in the office or **paralegals** spend time on the case, their time usually will be billed too. A paralegal is a person with specialized legal training who, although not a lawyer, assists the lawyer with legal tasks. Under a lawyer's supervision, a paralegal may do many of the same things a lawyer does, but in most states a paralegal may not represent a client in court.

A lawyer's secretary also helps the lawyer handle cases, but the secretary's time normally is not billed separately. (In some offices, if a secretary must work overtime because a case is on an expedited schedule or is unusually demanding, the secretary's time might be billed separately.)

In addition to fees for the lawyer's (and paralegal's) services, clients also usually pay **costs**. Costs are the out-of-pocket expenses that are associated with a case. Costs may include:

- **Court filing fees** (a fee paid to the court by a person who files a lawsuit or responds to one)

- **Fees to a process server** (who delivers papers to the opposing party advising the opposing party that a lawsuit has been filed)

- **Subpoena fees** (to persons who must appear in court or deliver documents to a party)

- **Court reporter fees** (to the court employee or private service that records court proceedings or **depositions** and then prepares a written transcript of what took place; a deposition is a procedure by which an attorney prepares for a possible trial by asking questions of a party or witness under oath)

- **Fees of experts** (for example, fees to an accountant to ascertain the value of a business or fees to a psychiatrist to conduct a custody evaluation)

- **Photocopying and telephone expenses** (particularly if the quantity of photocopying is large or if there are long-distance phone calls or faxes)

- **Travel expenses** (if the attorney must travel out of town in connection with the case)

Although most attorneys charge hourly rates, some will charge a fixed fee for handling an entire case. Attorneys who advertise that they will charge only a certain amount for a "simple divorce" (an amount often in the range of $250 to $600) usually mean that the stated amount will be the attorney's fee if the case is *very* simple. In other words, virtually nothing is contested and the paperwork is routine. If a case becomes more complicated, higher fees will be charged. The "costs" of a case (described above) usually are in addition to fees.

If a lawyer is not willing to enter into a fixed-fee arrangement, it is appropriate for the client to ask the attorney about the range of possible fees and costs and the factors that will make the fees higher or lower.

Many lawyers are reluctant to commit to a fixed fee, since the amount of effort necessary to handle a case can be difficult to predict at the beginning of a case, particularly if it is uncertain how many issues will be in dispute and how contentious the opposing side will be. In addition, use of an hourly fee, instead of a fixed fee, can control a client and limit expenses that are not cost-effective. If a client sees that fees are mounting, the client will be less likely to telephone the attorney over every small dispute or insist that the attorney expend substantial efforts regarding a piece of property that is worth a relatively small amount.

Attorneys in family law cases typically charge a **retainer** or an **advance on fees**. This, in effect, is a downpayment on the attorney's fees and costs. In some cases, the attorney may seek the entire fee up-front. If a case is handled for an amount less than the retainer or advance, the attorney should return the unused portion of the fee.

Contingency fees, like those used by attorneys who handle personal injury cases, generally are prohibited in family law cases. With a contingency fee, an attorney collects a fee only if a particular result is achieved, or, alternatively, the attorney may collect a portion of whatever monetary award is received by the client. Courts do not want to give attorneys a vested interest in a divorce. If, for example, an attorney were to receive a portion of whatever property award a client received in a divorce and the client wanted to reconcile with his or her spouse, the attorney could be in a position of opposing what was best for the client because the attorney wanted to receive a fee.

So contingency fees generally are prohibited in family law cases. An exception will be made in some states if the amount of money that is due a client is certain. If, for example, a client is owed a fixed amount in *past-due* child support or alimony, an attorney might be able to enter into a contingency fee to collect the past-due support, since there is only minimal likelihood of a conflict of interest related to the client's possible reconciliation.

If a client hires an attorney for representation beyond a consultation, most attorneys will give the client a written fee agreement stating the services that will be covered, the cost of services, and the times at which payment will be due. The client may choose to sign the agreement when it is presented, but it is quite permissible for the client to take the agreement home, read it over, and think about it before deciding whether to sign. In any case, the client should read the agreement carefully and ask the attorney any questions the client may have about the agreement.

In divorce cases, courts usually have the power to order one party to pay the other party's attorney fees. The basis for such cost shifting is a substantial difference in the income or property that each party has. If, for example, the husband earns a great deal more than the wife, the husband may be ordered to pay all or a portion of the wife's attorney's fees. If both parties have similar earning capacity or if both parties receive ample amounts of liquid assets as part of the divorce, the husband and wife are more likely to pay their own fees.

Another reason for having one party pay the other's party's legal fees is **bad faith** by the party from whom fees are sought. If one party does something he or she should not do (such as not paying child support or interfering with the other party's access to the child), the party who engaged in misconduct is likely to be ordered to pay the fees of the other party.

If one party has to pay the fees of the other party, that does not represent a blank check for the wronged party's attorney to bill any amount. The fees must be reasonable. A court can look at the facts of the case and decide what is a reasonable fee for the issue before the court.

HELPING THE LAWYER HELP YOU

Well-prepared clients help their cases go more smoothly. Clients can save time and money by gathering facts and carefully considering what goals they want achieve.

If property or support is contested, financial information usually must be gathered. A client can prepare inventories of the parties' assets and liabilities, itemizing the value or cost of each significant item, if known. Statements of the parties' income and expenses also are usually necessary. Useful places for the client (or attorney) to find financial information include copies of tax returns, checking account records, and charge records. If a client does not know certain information, the client can make lists of what is known, what is not known, and where more information might be located.

If either of the parties was divorced before, the client should try to obtain copies of the earlier divorce papers, particularly the marital settlement agreement and final order of the court.

If custody is at issue, the client could make lists of reasons why custody should be with the client. The reasons should be as specific as possible and include names, addresses, and telephone numbers of persons who might be able to testify in support of these arguments. The client should also list what their spouse's arguments are likely to be and what evidence the spouse would have in support of his or her position.

Divorce is a time of stress, and it probably will not be easy to methodically and logically gather information. But in taking steps to gain more control of one's current environment and future, the process can become therapeutic.

Although divorce is a time of stress, it also is a time to plan for the future. Clients should develop goals for the short term and the long term, and try to figure out how the issues of property, support, and time with children will fit into those goals. By identifying which issues are most important and which issues are less crucial, clients will help themselves and their attorneys resolve the problem in an orderly way while developing a reasonable plan for the future.

Many attorneys will ask their clients to fill out detailed questionnaires regarding finances and custody issues (if applicable). The forms should be filled out promptly and returned to the attorney. It will help the attorney organize the case and determine what information and arguments need to be developed.

Some attorneys will ask their clients to write a narrative statement about the marriage and divorce. The statement might include a description of:

1. significant events in the marriage
2. reasons for the divorce
3. child-raising responsibilities
4. contributions each party made to the marriage (financial, homemaking, or both)
5. good qualities and bad qualities about each party
6. the client's short-term and long-term goals and reasons for them
7. the client's perceptions of the spouse's short-term and long-term goals and the reasons for them

A written narrative may help the attorney and client understand the issues better. And writing the narrative may be cathartic for the client.

In the heat of a contested divorce, it may be tempting to be on the telephone with the attorney daily to blow off steam and seek advice. In most cases, that will not be an effective use of the attorney's time or the client's money. Usually it is best to save up a batch of inquiries and then discuss them with the attorney. If something urgent arises, such as the other party changing the residence of the children or hiding major assets, the attorney should be notified promptly.

Clients need to understand that attorneys are not always able to take client's calls immediately. Attorneys often are busy with trials or meetings with other clients. A well-organized attorney, however, will be able to return calls within twenty-four hours or will arrange for a staff member to call the client. Often, a client can pass on an inquiry or piece of information to the attorney's secretary or paralegal, who will discuss the matter with the attorney and then call the client back.

It is important for the client to be honest with the attorney. If there are skeletons in the closet (or a few loose bones) regarding finances, extramarital relationships, or other issues, it is best to be candid with the attorney about such matters so they can be dealt with if necessary. A client usually is worse off when adverse information comes up for the first time in the middle of a trial or the middle of negotiations, since the attorney may not be fully prepared to respond to the disclosures.

Family law attorneys hear many secrets of people's private lives. The attorney is not likely to be shocked or upset by the client's disclosure. Under rules of confidentiality, an attorney must keep a client's secrets. If a client reveals that he or she did something illegal in the past, the attorney must keep the secret. An attorney, however, cannot help a client pursue present or future illegal conduct. If the attorney has given information to the court or opposing side that the attorney later learns to be false, the attorney usually is obliged to correct the information.

In a bitter divorce, it is common for clients to want their attorney to act as an avenging angel—to make life miserable for their spouse and the spouse's attorney. That is not the proper function of the attorney. An attorney's job is to give calm, reasonable advice and to pursue the case in a diligent manner. Diligence and competence do not require antagonism or treating opposing counsel or the opposing party with disrespect.

An attorney who yells and screams is usually out of control and not serving the client's interest. The system of justice works better, and cases generally turn out better, when attorneys deal with each other (and with the court) in a civil manner.

DOCUMENTS TO ASSEMBLE

To help your lawyer analyze your case and give better advice, it can be helpful for you to assemble documents about your marriage. The documents can include:

- Tax returns (state and federal) for the last three years; perhaps earlier years as well
- Records of bank accounts—checking, savings, money market; certificates of deposit
- Investment account records
- Statements from pension plans or profit-sharing plans
- Recent pay stubs for yourself and spouse
- Credit card statements and records pertaining to other bills and expenses
- Deeds to home and other real estate; lease of apartment
- Automobile titles
- List and description of insurance policies—health, home, life, and disability
- Divorce decrees and settlement agreements from earlier marriages
- Résumés or curriculum vitae
- Written premarital agreement, if there was one
- Other documents you think are relevant

CHAPTER FIFTEEN

■

Mediation and
Other Alternatives

WORKING WITH LAWYERS AND COURTS is not the only way of resolving disputes. As people tire of the time, expense, and adversarial nature of litigation, both non-lawyers and lawyers have sought other means of solving problems. Methods of solving problems that do not involve going to court to have a judge decide the issue are referred to as **alternative dispute resolution (ADR)**.

Many methods of ADR are used in conjunction with court proceedings. For example, a couple seeking a divorce may use a mediator to help them resolve issues of custody, property, and support, but the couple still will need to go to court to have a judge enter an order officially ending the marriage.

There are several alternative ways of resolving family law disputes. Mediation is the most common. It will be discussed first, followed by advisory opinions, and arbitration.

MEDIATION

Mediation is a process by which the parties to a divorce (or some other dispute) try to resolve their disagreements outside of court with the help of a mediator. The mediator cannot force a settlement but tries to assist the parties to clarify their interests and work out their own solution.

In divorce actions, mediators often are involved in custody and visitation disputes. In some jurisdictions (particularly large urban areas), courts require mediation of custody and visitation disputes. The mother and father must talk with a court-appointed mediator to try to resolve the problem before putting their case before a judge. The mediator cannot force a resolution, but the parties can be told they must try mediation before coming to court to ask a judge to decide the issue. Court-ordered mediation usually is provided at no cost or at low cost to the parties (other than the cost of the filing fees required to initiate the court action).

Mediators can also handle property disputes and support disputes. A couple seeking mediation of disputes on financial issues probably will have to seek a private mediator, since most court-affiliated mediators deal with only custody and visitation issues.

If the parties resolve their disagreements through mediation, the attorneys for one or both of the parties still may be involved in finalizing and approving the agreement. Alternatively, if the parties feel comfortable working without attorneys and if they can get the paperwork right, they may draft their mediated settlement as an **agreed order** and take it to a judge for approval.

Most mediators are either mental health professionals or attorneys. Many mediators, particularly those associated with court mediation services, have degrees in social work or psychology. Private mediators (which the parties hire on their own) often are attorneys, although many are mental health professionals.

Mediators who are mental health professionals are not serving as therapists, and mediators who are attorneys are not serving as attorneys. Instead, they are professionals who are trying to help two (or more) people work out their differences.

Mediation often has the advantage of being cheaper and quicker than prolonged negotiations by attorneys or resolution of a case by a judge after a contested trial. A good mediator can help the parties build their problem-solving skills, and that can help them avoid later disputes. Most people who settle their cases through mediation leave the process feeling better than they would have if they had gone through a bitter court fight.

Mediation can have disadvantages, at least in certain cases. If, for example, the purpose of a mediation is to settle financial issues and one party is hiding assets or income, the other party might be better off with an attorney who can vigorously investigate the matter. Mediators usually are good at exploring the parties' needs, goals, and possible solutions, but they do not have the legal resources of an attorney to look for hidden information. A mediator, for example, cannot subpoena documents or witnesses to gather information.

Another problem with mediation can arise if one party is very passive and likely to be bulldozed by the other. In that situation, the mediated agreement might be lopsided in favor of the stronger party. A good mediator, however, will see to it that a weaker party's needs are expressed and protected. Some mediators may refuse to proceed with mediation if it looks as though one side will take improper advantage of the other.

Some legal and mental health professionals think that mediation is not appropriate if the case involves domestic violence. One concern is that mediation will give the abuser the opportunity to harm the victim again. Another concern is that victims of physical abuse are not able to adequately express and protect their own interests. However, other professionals believe that disputes in families with a history of domestic violence still can be mediated.

A final potential disadvantage of mediation is that if the mediation does not succeed, the parties may have wasted time and money on mediation and still face the expense of a trial.

There are not firm, nationwide figures regarding the percentage of cases that are resolved through mediation, but studies of mediation of custody disputes in several large cities report that between 50 and 90 percent of cases are settled through mediation.

ADVISORY OPINIONS

Instead of going to a formal trial before a judge, the parties and their attorneys may submit their cases to one or more experienced family law attorneys for an advisory opinion about how the case probably would be decided if it went to a court in the state. In effect, this is a mini-trial that is not binding.

With the clients present, the attorneys for the husband and wife make oral presentations and submit documents to the family law attorney. The amount of time for this "mini-trial" is set by agreement, but one to four hours is typical. After submission of "evidence," the family law attorney issues an opinion and the reasons for it. In many cases, the advisory opinion induces the parties to settle the case, although they still have the right to proceed to a trial before a judge.

In some cities, there is an established panel of attorneys who issue advisory opinions. The attorneys may hear cases and issue opinions at no charge or at a specified rate, depending on local custom. If there is not an established panel of family law attorneys to issue advisory opinions, clients and their attorneys still could seek out an attorney who would be willing to serve in such a capacity.

A variation on this approach is for the attorneys to talk to a judge before trial. The attorneys will lay out the essential facts and arguments of their case and ask the judge for an informal opinion. If the judge is willing, the judge may say something along the lines of, "If these are the facts that are proven at trial, here is how I am likely to decide . . . On the other hand, if this fact is different, my decision will be different . . ."

Some judges will allow clients to sit in on these meetings; others will not. The judge's decision to allow a client to sit in on such a meeting (sometimes called a **settlement conference**) may turn on the judge's perception of whether it will help the case or not. Judges do not want clients to become disruptive or emotionally upset at settlement conferences. In addition, some judges are concerned that if the client hears the judge say, "Here is how I am likely to decide the case (based on certain facts)," the client will assume the judge is prejudiced. In fact, a judge's comments at a settlement conference do not necessarily mean the judge is prejudiced. It usually just means that if the parties prove a certain set of facts, a certain result can be expected. If different facts are proved, the result would be different.

ARBITRATION

Another form of alternative dispute resolution is **arbitration**. Arbitration is not widely used in family law cases, but it is an option.

In arbitration, the parties agree to submit their dispute to a third party (other than a judge) for a binding decision. The arbitrator often is an attorney or a retired judge who hears the case—usually in a more expedited manner than a court would hear the case. Arbitration may be expedited in two respects. First, the arbitrator may be able to hear the case more quickly than a trial judge, particularly if the trial judge has a calendar crowded with many cases. Second, an arbitration may take fewer days than a trial, since arbitration procedures often are more informal than trials and the attorneys proceed more quickly. If the arbitration proceeds more quickly than a trial would proceed, arbitration will save time and costs.

Costs of arbitration vary, but are usually similar to attorneys' hourly rates (see pages 154 to 156).

In most states, husbands and wives are allowed to arbitrate issues of property and alimony, although this is not an area of law in which there are many court opinions specifically approving or disapproving the practice. In most states, however, courts are not likely to approve binding arbitration of custody and child support. Courts usually view themselves as ultimately responsible for protecting a child's welfare, and thus courts are reluctant to yield authority to an outside arbitrator.

In a New York case, for example, the mother and father agreed to have their marital disputes settled by a three-member rabbinical court that was serving as an arbitrator. The rabbinical court gave joint custody to the father and mother, but the state court declined to follow the decision. The state court viewed joint custody as not in the best interest of the children because of the "extreme antagonism" between the parents. The state court, however, **confirmed** (upheld) the rabbinical court's determination of maintenance.

WHERE TO GET MORE INFORMATION

ADOPTION

Your state may have a state adoption officer. These officials usually have offices in the state capital. The state government information operator can help you locate the officer for your state. For information about agency adoptions, contact:

The Child Welfare League of America
440 1st Street NW, Suite 310
Washington, DC 20001
(202) 638-2952

You also may wish to contact:

The National Committee for Adoption
1930 17th Street NW
Washington, DC 20009
(202) 328-1200

For information on independent adoption, check with your state, county, or city bar association. Ask if independent adoptions are legal in your state. Also ask if the bar association will refer you to lawyers who handle independent adoptions.

BATTERED SPOUSES

Many communities offer shelters for battered spouses and their children. Details on these shelters are available from the police, crisis intervention services, hospitals, churches, family or conciliation courts, local newspapers, or women's organizations. A national resource and referral service is:

The National Coalition Against Domestic Violence
P.O. Box 18749
Denver, CO 80218-0749
(303) 839-1852
Domestic Violence Hot Line: (800) 799-7233

The local or state chapter of the National Organization for Women (NOW) also should be able to provide information to help battered spouses.

CHILD SUPPORT

Every state has Regional Child Support Enforcement Units that help custodial parents establish and enforce child support orders and locate absent parents. (These offices are sometimes called IV-D Offices because they are required by Chapter IV-D of the Social Security Act.) You can locate the offices by looking under county or state government listings in the telephone book or by asking the state government switchboard.

Another resource is:

The Office of Child Support Enforcement Reference Center
Office of Child Support Enforcement
6110 Executive Boulevard
Rockville, MD 20852
(301) 217-7040

This office can help parents find their state's enforcement officers.

DIVORCE

Most local public libraries offer books about divorce. Ask the librarian for help. For information about how to find a family law attorney, see pages 151 to 154.

MEDIATION

A source for information on mediation is:

The Academy of Family Mediators
4 Militia Drive
Lexington, MA 02173
(617) 674-2663

The academy lists family mediators in every state by training and experience. Local courts (including the court clerk's office) also may have information regarding mediation services.

MISSING CHILDREN

Various agencies can offer help in finding children who are missing. They include:

Missing Children Help Center
410 Ware Boulevard, Suite 400
Tampa, FL 33619
(813) 623-KIDS or (800) USA-KIDS (toll-free)

or

National Center for Missing and Exploited Children
2101 Wilson Boulevard, Suite 550
Arlington, VA 22201
(800) 843-5678 (toll-free)

PENSIONS

One resource on pensions is the U.S. Department of Labor. The address is:

Pension and Welfare Benefits Administration
U.S. Department of Labor, Division of Technical Assistance and
    Inquiries
Room N5658
200 Constitution Avenue NW
Washington, DC 20210
(202) 254-7013

The Pension Rights Center informs employees of their rights involving pensions. This private organization also offers booklets that explain related topics.

Pension Rights Center
918 16th Street NW, Suite 704
Washington, DC 20006
(202) 296-3776

SOCIAL SECURITY

Your local Social Security Administration office can provide information and literature on benefits. You can find its address and telephone number in your local telephone directory—usually under "U.S. Government."

TAXES

The basic resource on federal income taxes is the Internal Revenue Service (IRS). You can find your regional office in the phone book under "U.S. Government." You also may wish to contact an accountant or a tax lawyer.

Free publications on family taxes available from the IRS include *Community Property and the Federal Income Tax* (Publication 555), *Tax Information for Divorced or Separated Individuals* (Publication 504), and *Tax Rules for Children and Dependents* (Publication 929).

WOMEN'S ISSUES

You can receive a free list of publications from:

The Legal Defense and Education Fund of the National Organization
    for Women (NOW)
99 Hudson Street
New York, NY 10013
(212) 925-6635

INDEX

ABOUT THE AUTHOR

■

JEFF ATKINSON is an adjunct professor at DePaul University College of Law in Chicago, Illinois. Professor Atkinson has taught a variety of subjects, including family law. He also serves as a professor-reporter for the Illinois Judicial Conference, responsible for training Illinois judges in family law and legal ethics. He is author of a two-volume treatise entitled *Modern Child Custody Practice,* published by the Michie Company of Charlottesville, Virginia. He is former chair of the ABA's Child Custody Committee and is a member of the editorial board of the ABA's *Family Advocate,* a quarterly magazine for lawyers and judges. In addition, Professor Atkinson serves on the governing council of the ABA's Section of Family Law.